Last Wills

Includes Living Wills

MADE E-Z PRODUCTS™ Inc.
Burnaby, B.C./service@CanadaForms.com

Last Will and Testament
© Copyright 2001 C.G.T. Canadian Legal Forms Ltd

P.O. Box 82664
Burnaby, B.C. V5C 5W4

service@CanadaForms.com

1 2 3 4 5 6 7 8 9 10

This publication is designed to provide accurate and authoritative information in regard to subject matter covered. It is sold with the understanding that neither the publisher nor author is engaged in rendering legal, accounting, or other professional services. If legal advice or other expert assistance is required, the services of a competent professional should be sought.

Last Will and Testament

Important Notice

Table of Contents

How to use this guide 6

Introduction 7

Last Will and Testament

1. You need a last will 11

2. Types of wills 27

3. Will contests 33

4. The Executor/Executrix/Trustee 41

5. Preparing your will 57

6. Will provisions 75

7. Planning your funeral 91

8. Instructions for completing your will 101

Living Will

9. What is a living will? 111

10. Your power of attorney for personal care 117

11. Euthanasia 131

12. Provincial laws 137

13. Preparing your living will 159

Estate Planning

14. What is estate planning? 171

15. Protecting your assets 177

16. Trusts and life insurance 193

The forms in this guide 205

Glossary of useful terms 227

Index 233

How to use this guide

C.G.T. Canadian Legal Forms, Ltd. can help you achieve an important legal objective conveniently, efficiently and economically. But it is important to properly use this guide if you are to avoid later difficulties.

- Carefully read all information, warnings and disclaimers concerning the legal forms in this guide. If after thorough examination you decide that you have circumstances that are not covered by the forms in this guide, or you do not feel confident about preparing your own documents, consult a lawyer.

- Complete each blank on each legal form. Do not skip over inapplicable blanks or lines intended to be completed. If the blank is inapplicable, mark "N/A" or "None" or use a dash. This shows you have not overlooked the item.

- Always use pen or type on legal documents—never use pencil.

- Avoid erasures and "cross-outs" on final documents. Use photocopies of each document as worksheets, or as final copies. All documents submitted to the court must be printed on one side only.

- Correspondence forms may be reproduced on your own letterhead if you prefer.

- Whenever legal documents are to be executed by a partnership or corporation, the signatory should designate his or her title.

- It is important to remember that on legal contracts or agreements between parties all terms and conditions must be clearly stated. Provisions may not be enforceable unless in writing. All parties to the agreement should receive a copy.

- Instructions contained in this guide are for your benefit and protection, so follow them closely.

- Always keep legal documents in a safe place and in a location known to your spouse, family, Executor/ Executrix/Trustee or lawyer.

Introduction

You work most of your adult life, and build an estate. Eventually, you wish to bequeath that estate to friends and relatives.

Like planning a wedding, birthday party, or anniversary, you must be organized and prepared. Without adequate preparation, your hard-earned property and the welfare of your loved ones are at stake. As you will see, even the government can enter your private life if you do not take the necessary steps.

As you age, your health may fail you, and you might not be able to make medical decisions for yourself. Medical technology can prolong your life longer under circumstances you may not want. Your loved ones are financially dependent upon you. How can you effectively communicate your wishes and desires under these conditions—how can you protect yourself, your property and your loved ones?

All this involves the process of estate planning where you plan your financial future complete with the essential documents that ensure your wishes are implemented after your death. A last will and testament is the most common estate planning document. It allows you to leave your property to whom you wish. The living will enables you to exercise your right to die with dignity—instead of prolonging it artificially—when you can no longer speak for yourself. And finally, the power of attorney for health care designates someone to make medical decisions for you when you are incapable of doing so.

The information and forms contained in this book assist you in making the necessary provisions for you and your loved ones—without a lawyer. Achieve peace of mind knowing that your next of kin are provided for, and by making your wishes regarding health care known.

Last Will
and
Testament

You need a last will

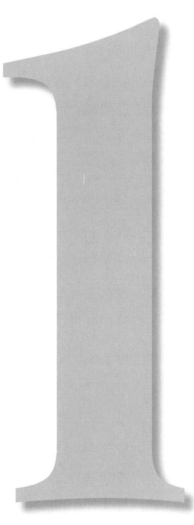

You need a last will

In its simplest terms, a will is a formal, legally enforceable statement of how you wish to dispose of your property upon your death. The person(s) who inherit your property are your *beneficiaries*. A valid will allows your last wishes to be protected and enforced by provincial law.

Because it can be changed at any time prior to your death, your will can be used to express a variety of emotions: kindness, anger, surprise, appreciation, etc. Wills also may be used to stimulate others to act, to express compassion, to provide the means to decide, to get revenge, to surprise beneficiaries, and to show appreciation for hard work and loyalty.

Why a will is important

A will is the simplest form of an estate plan. It is also the most important document of any estate plan, since it is the one item that makes clear what you want done with the things you leave behind.

> **HINT** Without a valid will you cannot control who will inherit your property upon your death.

Most married people, who have children or not, leave their entire estate to their surviving spouse. Should you die *intestate* (without a will), your property will be distributed according to provincial law, which is likely to be inconsistent with your personal wishes. The law may demand that your property be given to distant relatives for whom you have little or no feeling, instead of to a good friend and neighbor of 20 years whom you would choose to inherit your property.

Even if you believe that you have nothing of value, a will can:

- cover an unexpected inheritance

- cover an accident claim

- cover a wrongful death award

With a will you can:

- determine precisely who will inherit your property

- designate who will administer your estate

- designate who will act as guardian for your minor children should they be left without a surviving parent

- assign your personal belongings, such as memorabilia and family heirlooms, to whom you designate

- carry out your wishes regarding burial, cremation, and funeral services

- avoid costly and lengthy estate litigation

If you fail to provide in your will for your common-law spouse or fail to make a will, he or she will be treated as a complete stranger and thus may be entitled to nothing.

Intestacy

Unfortunately, people often delay preparing their wills. Some may dread the discussion of death. Some feel their estates are not large enough to require a will. Some feel they don't have the time to prepare a will.

Intestacy, or dying intestate, means dying without a valid will. All provinces have a fixed formula for distributing your property should you die intestate. The laws that govern the distribution of property of such an estate are known as the *Laws of Intestate Succession*. Intestate succession means the order of which heirs receive the estate of someone who has died without a will.

The *Laws of Intestate Succession* have different names in each province, but the distribution is basically the same when:

- There is only a remaining spouse

- There are only remaining children

- There is no spouse or children

The laws vary when both children and a spouse are involved.

The *Laws of Intestate Succession* are provincial laws applied in exactly the same way to all estates that are not governed by wills. These laws determine who your beneficiaries, your administrator, and the guardian of your children will be. This means you will have absolutely no say in the distribution of your property after your death.

If you die intestate, your surviving spouse automatically inherits a certain percentage of your estate. This is called the *preferential share*. That percentage differs from province to province, depending upon whom your other surviving relatives are. Any and all surviving parents, children, grandchildren or other descendants will affect how your estate's assets are divided. Again, you have absolutely no say in how your assets will be distributed if you leave no valid will.

For example, Bruce and Helen had a sizeable jointly held estate, a home in Alberta and no children together or living parents. Neither had found the time or realized the importance of preparing wills. Bruce died first, followed a few days later by Helen. The Alberta law of intestacy, the Intestate Succession Act, distributed all of the jointly held property to Helen's brother, whom Bruce hated. Unfortunately, Bruce's three children from a previous marriage received none of Bruce's jointly held assets.

Dying intestate may be even more catastrophic when you are a common-law or same-sex couple living together. In the case of a common-law spouse, your partner cannot inherit any part of your estate upon your death unless he or she was financially dependent on you before your death (depending on provincial law). Current intestate and succession laws do not provide at all for surviving partners of same-sex couples.

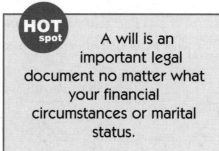

HOT spot A will is an important legal document no matter what your financial circumstances or marital status.

Intestate Succession

Who inherits what if you have no will? The Laws of Intestate Succession, drafted by each province, determine who is to inherit.

The Intestate Succession Act is valid in the provinces of:

- Alberta

- Manitoba

- Newfoundland

- Northwest Territories and Nunavut

- Nova Scotia

- Saskatchewan

- Yukon

The province of British Columbia adheres to the *Estate Administration Act*, Ontario recognizes the *Succession Law Reform Act*, Prince Edward Island applies the *Probate Act*, and New Brunswick enforces the *Devolution of Estates Act*.

What happens to your property?

Personal property

There are two types of personal property: tangible and intangible. Tangible property is anything, other than real estate, that can be physically touched.

Automobiles, computers, books, furniture, silverware, tools, coin and stamp collections, clothing and other personal effects are common examples of tangible property. Identify and describe such gifts in your will by title, serial, or I.D. number. You may bypass probate (the legal process governing the distribution of an estate) and facilitate the transfer of such property by having joint title (with right of survivorship) with your beneficiary. Joint title with right of survivorship means that ownership is held in two names, and upon death of one owner, the other owner becomes the sole owner of the property. Remember, when you have joint title to tangible property, the co-owner's consent is necessary in order to sell or exchange it. Similarly, the co-owner would be responsible for any outstanding liens or debts on the property upon your death.

Tangible personal property has two types of value: cash value and sentimental value. Generally, the cost to replace this type of property is more than the amount of money you would receive if you sold it. For example, observe the cost of items at an estate sale. This factor may alter your thinking regarding your bequests. You may decide to give a relatively new stereo system and video recorder to a niece and nephew when you are alive rather than sell the items and have them divide the money after your death. You may also decide to give your old jewelry to a daughter when you are still able to explain what it means to you.

Intangible personal property consists of stocks, bonds, drafts and notes. These types of properties are considered intangible because they represent your ownership of something else. For example, a check is intangible because it only represents your money, but it is not your money itself. These are considered liquid assets because they may be converted to cash quickly without loss in value. Because of their liquidity, assets such as cash, checking, savings, and money market accounts make excellent bequests. Stocks, bonds, and other financial investments may also be converted to cash but their value depends on when they are converted. Intangible property also includes intellectual property such as copyrights, patents, licenses, and residual performance rights.

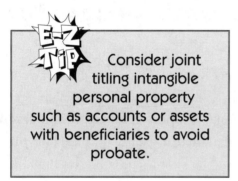

Consider joint titling intangible personal property such as accounts or assets with beneficiaries to avoid probate.

Because it is not as liquid, leave intangible property such as stock in privately held corporations, limited and regular partnership shares, and private notes directly to your beneficiaries rather than selling them beforehand and leaving the cash equivalent in your will. This permits the beneficiary to decide upon the most advantageous time to sell these instruments.

You may leave all or part of your shares to your beneficiaries. When you leave a specific number of shares to a beneficiary, and the dividends from these shares are reinvested as additional shares, these additional shares become part of your estate and must be distributed. You can avoid this by bequeathing all of the shares to your beneficiary.

You may bequeath both tangible and intangible property in your will. You may leave the particular property to specific individuals or you may bequeath your entire estate to one person. Sometimes, you may utilize other techniques instead of a will to transfer property such as joint titling (with right of survivorship), tax-exempt lifetime gifts, or trusts.

Intellectual property, like other forms of intangible property, also may be bequeathed in your will. Royalties earned from such intellectual properties as patents and copyrights may comprise a significant portion of your estate. When you share intellectual property rights with a business partner, you only may bequeath *your* percentage to your beneficiaries.

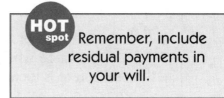

Specify the patent or copyright identification number in your will when leaving intellectual property rights. Also, account for any residual payments you currently receive. For example, if you were an actress in a successful TV show whose reruns are currently aired, you would receive residual payments.

Real property

Real property consists of land and any improvements to it. The categories of real property include unimproved property (forests, marshes and vacant lots), residential property (primary residence, second home, lot and mobile home, co-op, condominium, and time-share unit), and income-producing property (farm, campground, commercial, and hotel). When leaving real property in your will, refer to its street address, city, province, and country, if applicable. When the property is rural or unimproved, specify its tax number or lot/tract number. Locate the legal description of the property in the deed.

Income-producing property, unlike intangible and tangible property, requires active management to continue the income stream. For example, owning a farm or an apartment building necessitates upkeep and decision making. When your primary beneficiary is incapable or unwilling to manage these properties, their value may diminish. When you own and manage commercial or rental property, draft a special document in which you specify an individual or firm to manage your property upon your death. Make reference to this document in your will. You may appoint an agent or firm to manage the property in one document, and transfer the ownership and income to a beneficiary in your will. Sign a binding agreement with your prospective agent or firm clearly outlining terms and compensation.

Because provincial laws vary widely, it is possible for your real estate, located within your province, to be transferred differently from your real estate located outside of your province. Without a valid will, the transfer of your real property may be subject to untimely delays and additional expenses. This is due to the court's need to issue directives instead of following the instructions that would have been contained in your will. These directives may demand that someone supply the court with a full account of your estate's assets, debts, and beneficiaries. The more complicated the estate, the more time and money it will take in the form of extra court costs.

> **note** The laws of the province where the real estate is located determine how your real property will be distributed if there is no will.

The administrator

When you die intestate, the provincial court selects an Administrator to distribute your estate according to the intestacy laws in your province. This process can take a long time especially when more than one individual wants the position. In addition, added costs for an Administrator bond may be required. This bond acts as an insurance policy to cover any errors the

Administrator may make. The court chooses the Administrator according to the following order:

- Spouse

- Child or Grandchild

- Siblings

Perhaps, you would have appointed someone else if you had a will. In addition, the delay of the appointment of the Administrator leaves your estate with no one to handle its assets or make timely decisions. If you owned a business, no one else may manage it until an Administrator is appointed, and family members might fight for control of your company.

In addition, your estate may lose profits from selling investments at the right time because no one is available to act on your behalf. Even when the Administrator is selected, his or her investment decisions will still be restricted by your province's *Trustee Act*. In some provinces, this Act provides a list of viable investments. This list might prevent the Administrator from investing in a manner that would be most beneficial to your heirs. He or she might be forced to sell an investment when market conditions are bad or need to acquire the court's approval to refrain from selling—translating into more costs.

note Some provinces have enacted a "prudent investor" rule, which allows the chosen Administrator to make the best investments possible.

Some provincial intestacy laws obligate your heirs to pay from your estate a specific amount of money to your spouse or children. When you do not leave enough cash to fulfill this requirement, your heirs must sell other assets from your estate, perhaps your treasured vacation home that provided fond memories for your family. Avoid these scenarios by preparing a will.

When you have a spouse

In each province, if you are married, have no children and die intestate, your husband or wife will inherit your entire estate. Even when you leave parents, siblings, or nieces and nephews in addition to your spouse, your spouse will receive everything. (except in Quebec where these relatives are entitled to a share of your estate). Remember, in most provinces, only a spouse married legally may inherit your estate. Therefore, if you have lived with someone for several years, but are not legally married, you must prepare a will. Why? Because if you die intestate, your surviving partner may receive nothing.

When you are married and have children

If you die intestate, and leave both a spouse and children behind, both your spouse and children will receive portions of the estate. The percentage of the share of the estate that each family member will inherit varies from province to province. In some provinces, the spouse receives more than the children, while in others, the children receive more than the spouse. In some provinces, your spouse will receive a fixed amount (a "preferential share"), and the remainder is split among your spouse and children *per stirpes*. *Per stirpes* literally means "through your descendants." When one of your children dies before you, his or her children (your grandchildren) divide their parent's share (your child) equally among them. For a further discussion and example of *per stirpes* bequests, see Debts, Chapter 6 and page 80.

In some provinces, the surviving spouse has the right to inherit the family home in lieu of, or as a portion of, the preferential share. In other provinces, your spouse may have rights to a share of the family home plus the preferential share.

Many provinces institute family law statutes that may influence the amount of your spouse's portion of your estate. He or she may elect to receive the portion allowed under the family law statute if it is a greater amount than under the intestacy law.

When you are not married with children

Nowadays, it is not uncommon to have children but no spouse. Your spouse may have died, you may be divorced, or you may be living together but not legally married. When you die intestate under these circumstances, your children inherit your estate equally. In many provinces, your partner, if you have one, will not receive anything as you were not legally married.

In this case, note the importance of preparing a will. Would you intentionally leave nothing to your mate if he or she was living with you, especially if he or she was the father or mother of your children? Even if your children were from a previous marriage, you may still want to leave something to your mate. Consider these circumstances when you are not legally married but have children.

If you are single and childless

When you die intestate, if you have no living spouse, are legally divorced or have never married, and have no children, your other relatives will be in line to inherit your estate.

According to the following order, your estate will be given to:

1) Both your parents, if they are still living or to the surviving parent

2) Your siblings if both parents are deceased. If any of your siblings are deceased, their interest will be apportioned per stirpes among their children (your nieces and nephews)

3) Grandparents, aunts, uncles, and cousins, when you do not have any siblings or nieces and nephews

4) The provincial government, if you have no living relatives. This process is called *escheat*.

Consider the consequences

Now, ask yourself the following questions:

- *Are you married with minor children?*

  If you are, you may want to leave your entire estate to your spouse to manage family finances as she or he deems best. However, when you die intestate, your spouse may inherit only one-third of your estate, according to the law in your province, and your children will obtain the remainder. In addition, your minor children's shares will be handled by the provincial government rather than your spouse.

- *Do you have a life partner, companion or mate to whom you are not legally married?*

  Regardless of the nature of the relationship or whether you live with each other, your partner has no legal claim to your estate. He or she will receive nothing.

- *Are you separated?*

  If you are not yet divorced and die suddenly intestate, in a majority of the provinces your "ex" will have the right to a significant portion of, if not your entire estate.

- *Do you have dear friends about whom you care?*

  If you are single and don't have family ties, might you not help a struggling friend, reward someone who has been there for you in good and bad times, or simply leave something of yours for them that you know they would appreciate and to remember you by? Obviously, you need a will for these circumstances as provincial intestacy law does not recognize friends.

- *Do you wish to make a charitable contribution?*

  It may not be possible to leave money to your alma mater or any other organization that you believe in without making a will.

- *Are you married and have children from a previous marriage?*

  Without a will, your hard-earned money could wind up in the possession of your current spouse's children instead of your own.

Types of wills

Types of wills

There are seven basic wills recognized by Canadian law. Although not valid in every province, each will has its own set of requirements.

These are the basic wills recognized by Canadian law:

1) **Holographic Wills** are handwritten, dated, and signed only by the person making the will (the testator). It is not witnessed. Any written but unwitnessed will is considered extremely unreliable and often does not stand up in court. A holographic will needs no witnesses, but is not valid in British Columbia and Nova Scotia. Some other provinces may accept them even if unsigned if it is in the handwriting of the testator. Others require a signature. A will that is typewritten (or on a printed will form) and signed by the testator is not considered a holographic will because it is not handwritten, and it is not a conventional will because it lacks witnesses.

2) **Reciprocal Wills** are used when spouses designate each other as beneficiaries. Each contains an agreement that neither testator will make any changes in his or her will after the death of the other. Spouses using reciprocal wills should also designate an alternative or contingent beneficiary. To avoid confusion, it is best to define all of the terms and conditions of your will as clearly as possible. Simply make two completely separate wills that are identical, yet name each other as beneficiaries.

3) **Conventional or "bread and butter" Wills** are the most common type of will. They are recognized by every province in Canada and must meet the following requirements:

- They must be in writing (verbal or videotaped wills are not acceptable).

- The testator must be of legal age.

- It must be signed by the testator at the end of the will.

- The testator must sign in front of at least two witnesses who must in turn, and after the testator has signed, sign in front of each other and the testator.

- The witnesses must be of legal age and cannot be a named beneficiary or spouse of the deceased.

It is not required but recommended that you date the document. The testator and the witnesses must initial each page.

4) **International Wills** are wills which must meet a number of formalities outlined by The Convention Providing a Uniform Law on the Form of an International Will which met in 1973. The province of last residence must have accepted the Convention. Also, it stipulates certain conditions associated with the writing of the will, witnesses and administration. Not all provinces accept this type of will.

5) **Serviceman or Privileged Wills** are for members of the armed forces or mariners. This type of will is the same as the conventional will without the witnesses. They do not have to be signed by the testator but can be signed by another person in his or her presence or not signed at all. However, some provinces require another witness in the case of a will signed by a third party. Minors

employed by the service can write a valid serviceman's will. These wills are valid beyond the term of service but are only valid if made while on active service, or if a seaperson, while at sea or in the course of a voyage.

6) **Notarial Wills**, legal only in Quebec, are wills created by notaries who are given will-making powers in the Civil Code of Quebec.

7) **Conditional Wills** occur when a document that is intended to be a will is conditional on an event that takes place before the testator's death. This type of will is not considered a will. Most importantly, a will is always revocable even if it states "irrevocable."

Who can make a will?

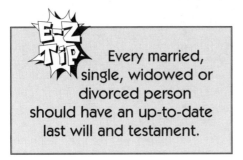

E-Z TIP

Every married, single, widowed or divorced person should have an up-to-date last will and testament.

The person whose will it is, is called the *Testator*. The only qualifications are that you be of legal age and sound mind. An adult is one who has reached the following minimum ages:

Alberta	18
British Columbia	19
New Brunswick	19
Manitoba	18
Newfoundland	17
Northwest Territories	19

Nova Scotia	19
Ontario	18
Prince Edward Island	18
Quebec	18
Saskatchewan	18
Yukon Territory	19

Minors generally cannot make their own wills, as they are not deemed competent. If you are a minor, you need an attorney to prepare a will. Property owned by a minor is thus held "in trust" by a parent or other designated guardian. The parent or guardian should therefore consider the testamentary wishes of a minor whose assets they control.

Will contests

3

Will contests

Under certain circumstances, a will may be contested by a beneficiary or heir. To contest a will, the person must prove that he or she would lose a benefit if the will was allowed.

Challenging a will

Grounds for contesting a will include proving:

- that the will was not properly filled out

- that the testator was of unsound mind

- that there was fraud involved

- that the testator acted contrary to his or her real wishes and desires

- that the testator did not adequately provide for a dependent (dependent is defined differently in different provinces, but includes spouse and children)

You must be of sound mind when you prepare and sign the will. Sound mind simply means that you must understand what you are giving

HOT spot The burden of proof is always upon the person contesting the will.

away and to whom you are giving it. You must also prepare your will free from implied or actual threats, pressure, trickery, undue influence, or other fraud.

note Even evidence of mental illness or ongoing psychiatric care does not automatically prevent you from preparing a valid will.

Simple absent-mindedness or forgetfulness is not evidence of mental illness. Should you have a history of serious mental disorders, it may be wise to consult with a qualified medical practitioner just prior to preparing your will. This will help establish your competency and be useful should your will later be contested on the grounds of mental incompetency.

As a general guideline, to meet the test for testamentary capacity, the testator must:

1) understand that he or she is making a will and a will disposes of property on death

2) be aware of his or her assets being disposed of and understand the nature and extent of his or her property

3) give proper consideration to those who have an appropriate claim upon the estate

4) be free of delusions which may affect his or her decisions

Your legal and financial obligations

Before preparing your will, be aware that each province has legislation to defend the interests of a spouse and dependants. Your legal and financial duties to your family endure beyond your death, and influence your liberty to bequeath assets in your will. This is known as the "restriction on testamentary freedom." A dependant is considered an individual who needed you for his or her financial support just prior to your death. Examples of dependents are your spouse and children. In some provinces, such as Prince Edward Island and Ontario, the law recognizes a common-law spouse, parents, and grandchildren as dependants. It is necessary to understand your legal and financial obligations so that your will is not contested.

Providing for dependents

Laws in many provinces protect dependents by allowing them to petition the courts to acquire an order against the estate for continued support. The Family Relief Act (Alberta), the Dependents Relief Act (Manitoba), the Wills Variation Act (British Columbia), the Dependents of a Deceased Person Relief Act (Prince Edward Island), and the Succession Law Reform Act (Ontario) cover the rights of dependents. The language and title of the various acts differ from province to province, but the purpose is identical. Each province delegates to the courts the power to demand the estate to furnish support to dependents if they have not adequately been provided for in the will.

note Your will may be contested in court if you do not provide sufficient relief in your will for your dependents.

The order for maintenance and support may be derived from the assets of the estate and consists of:

- a yearly or annual stipend either on a temporary or permanent basis, or until the dependent reaches a certain age, or until a specific occasion such as marriage

- a set amount to be placed in trust

- real estate to be placed in trust for a short or extended period of time

- ownership of specific property for short- or long-term

- any other manner the court deems suitable

When the order is granted, it overrules the directions in your will, and can modify the allotment of the estate. More requirements may be contained in a marriage contract or separation agreement.

Common-law couples

The federal Income Tax Act provides common-law partners rights like those for married couples. Real estate, RRSPs, and RRIFs may be assigned to a common-law spouse and the income tax delayed until the surviving spouse dies. However, common-law spouses are not entitled to property by law, but they may have a case for continued support if they were financially dependent on you immediately before your death.

To provide for a common-law partner and protect yourself you may:

- hold property jointly

- designate each other as the beneficiary in your respective wills, for life insurance policies, RRSPs and RRIFs

- designate each as the other's attorney-in-fact

- draft a co-habitation agreement and include the distribution of property and support upon separation and death

Same-sex couples

While the number of same-sex partners has grown, lawmakers are considering changing present legislation to grant new estate planning rights to this growing minority. In fact, in Ontario a same-sex partner may qualify for ongoing support if he or she was financially dependent on his her partner before death. While it is difficult to assess their nature and when they might become effective, expect that:

- Pension benefits will cover all members of public and private pension plans, if you name your partner as your beneficiary

- CPP survivor benefits will be furnished to same-sex couples

- Same-sex couples will have to obey the same tax regulations as common-law couples

As current law generally does not recognize property rights for common-law couples upon death or separation unless they are financially dependent, it is unknown whether same-sex couples will be granted these rights in provinces other than Ontario. As we have mentioned before, if you are involved in a same-sex relationship or are part of an unmarried couple, be specific with your bequests in your will—your partner will not be protected under current intestacy laws. In fact, to be on the safe side, do the following:

- Draft wills and provide specific instructions

- Draft a co-habitation agreement

- Designate your partner as your beneficiary on RRSPs/RRIFs, life insurance, stocks, and pension plans

- Designate your partner as your attorney-in-fact

- Maintain assets as joint tenants with rights of survivorship (except in Quebec)

- Consider creating a living trust immediately before death

Matrimonial possessions

Some provinces have legislation that defends a spouse's right to a fair and reasonable share of property (for example, the home). You can not write your spouse out of the will or leave him or her less than he or she would have acquired under the terms of a divorce.

Divorce

Depending upon the terms of your divorce agreement, sometimes support payments end at death. Other divorce agreements stipulate the purchase and continuation of life insurance to furnish funds for dependents after you die. Some divorce agreements do not address the issue at all. However, you must abide by the terms of your divorce agreement regarding dependent support as these terms overrule your will's directions.

note If you were divorced and furnishing support to your ex-spouse and/or children under a divorce agreement, you may have to maintain these payments after your death.

The Executor/ Executrix/ Trustee

The Executor/ Executrix/ Trustee

You must name an Executor/Executrix/Trustee for your estate and authorize your Executor/Executrix/ Trustee to probate your estate and carry out the provisions of your will. This person makes the important administrative decisions, gathers the assets, and distributes them to the beneficiaries after your death. The Executor/Executrix/Trustee is sometimes called the executor or administrator if a male, and the executrix or administratrix, if a female.

By taking the time to prepare your will, you have the advantage of naming your own Executor/Executrix/Trustee.

Failure to name an Executor/ Executrix/Trustee does not invalidate your will. However, the court will try to find a relative who is willing to administer your estate. This can be a time-consuming and fruitless process, possibly resulting in the court appointing a distant relative, with no skill, over a good friend to administer your affairs. If you leave no will at all, the court again appoints a relative to take charge of your affairs. This relative could be a virtual stranger. He or she may be completely unaware of and unbounded by your last wishes, and distribute your property according to provincial law.

What to look for

Since the primary duty of your Executor/Executrix/Trustee is to carry out the terms of your will, he or she must be someone responsible. You are trusting this person to act in the best interest of your estate. Typically, a spouse, relative or close friend serves as Executor/Executrix/Trustee, as the duties are not difficult and your Executor/Executrix/ Trustee will retain an attorney to process the necessary probate forms.

> **HOT spot**
> The primary concern in selecting an Executor/Executrix/ Trustee is that he or she be reliable and trustworthy in carrying out your specific wishes.

An Executor/Executrix/Trustee must be over 18 years of age. You should appoint someone who is close to your age or younger to ensure that he or she outlives you and can carry out your wishes.

Do not choose a minor, a convicted felon or someone unwilling to serve. Eliminate anyone who might have a conflict of interest. The court will pay close attention to this point. For example, do not choose your business partner if he or she will have to evaluate the assets of your share of the business.

It is also important that your Executor/Executrix/Trustee live in the same province that you live in. Sometimes a bank representative is named Executor/Executrix/Trustee for an estate, but fees for this service tend to be high.

Sometimes a testator names two people as his or her Executor/Executrix/Trustee. Sometimes a lot of conflict is avoided by having joint Executors/Executrices and Trustees so that a power struggle does not ensue between a beneficiary and Executor/Executrix/Trustee.

Some provinces require the Executor/Executrix/Trustee to be a permanent resident of that province. Others allow the appointment of nonresidents if they are relatives of the testator. Therefore, you should not appoint a non-resident of your province as your Executor/Executrix/Trustee without first checking your province's applicable laws.

Always check in advance with your proposed Executor/Executrix/ Trustee, who must be of legal age, to be certain he or she is willing to serve. If an Executor/Executrix/Trustee refuses to serve, "renunciation" occurs.

Always name an alternate Executor/Executrix/Trustee in the event the named Executor/Executrix/Trustee shall, for any reason, be unable to serve. This is especially important for large estates.

Consider selecting a professional executor such as a trust company, an accountant, or a lawyer when:

- You foresee battles for possession of your assets or business

- You don't trust anyone you know to handle the responsibilities of the Executor/Executrix/Trustee

- You cannot find anyone willing to serve in that capacity

- You have assets that will be tied up in trust for several years and do not want to burden friends or family

- You have complicated financial and family concerns such as business income, foreign property, and various investments

If you plan to appoint a professional executor, be sure you understand:

- How he or she will be compensated

- What information he or she will supply your beneficiaries

- How often he or she will consult with your beneficiaries

- How he or she will work with your co-executor, if you name one

If you cannot decide whether to select a professional or family member as your Executor/Executrix/Trustee, consider designating a family member to be co-executor with the professional. The family member can deal with the family conflicts, and the professional can undertake the administrative and legal chores. If you choose this arrangement, select the primary decision maker or, if you prefer, state that they must make joint decisions, and the professional must execute the administrative tasks.

Many people choose a trust company in their will to be Executor/Executrix/Trustee. The advantages of employing a trust company as your Executor/Executrix/Trustee are as follows:

- **Knowledge and understanding of wills and estate planning.** A trust company can offer advice on minimizing taxes for your beneficiaries, and estate distribution.

- **Long-term service**. Selection of a trust company guarantees coverage for the full time required to administer the estate. When you establish a trust for young children, the trust must be maintained until the children reach legal age. This may take many years—longer than a non-professional Executor/Executrix/Trustee may be willing to serve.

- **Availability.** Your trust officer will be able to answer any questions your beneficiaries may have.

- **Complete focus on the estate's requirements.** When you appoint a family member or friend to be your Executor/ Executrix/Trustee, he or she often has other responsibilities and cannot devote as much time to his or her role as your Executor/Executrix/Trustee as a trust company can.

- **Financial management.** A trust company can manage your estate's investments such as your assets or your business until it is the time to sell them.

- **Supplying funds.** A trust company can provide for your family's urgent financial needs after your death.

- **Maintaining a neutral bias.** Everyone has heard stories of families fighting over a will. One child may resent that the other one was appointed Executor/Executrix/Trustee. Another child may be upset that he or she did not receive as much money or property as another. Two daughters may fight over a piece of jewelry that you forgot to bequeath in your will. The possibilities are endless. You can avoid these scenarios by appointing a trust company to act as a neutral party in resolving potential conflicts.

- **Reducing stress.** When you hire a trust company as your Executor/Executrix/Trustee, you obtain peace of mind knowing that your estate will be handled by a competent professional with experience and expertise. This psychological security may make the estate planning process easier and less anxiety-ridden.

However, be aware of the disadvantages of trust companies:

- **High fees.** Their fees are reasonable only for larger estates, i.e., at least $500,000 gross assets.

- **Long distance location.** As banks have bought all the prominent trust companies, the trust companies have since been downsized and centralized. Trust companies with estate planning departments are no longer located in every city. To speak with your trust officer you or your beneficiaries may have to rely on an 800 number only to find an office located far away.

Duties of the Executor/Executrix/Trustee

To help you choose your Executor/Executrix/Trustee and, perhaps, to make it easier for that person to serve, the following are some of the typical duties and responsibilities of the position:

- Keep assets in the estate

- Receive assets from others

- Perform or refuse to perform the decedent's contracts

- Fulfill charitable pledges made by the decedent

- Deposit or invest the estate's assets in appropriate investments

- Acquire, abandon or sell assets of the estate

- Make repairs, erect or demolish buildings

- Subdivide, develop or improve land

- Lease from or to others with an option to purchase

- Enter into a mineral lease or similar agreement

- Vote securities in person or by proxy

- Insure assets against damage, loss and liability

- Insure himself or herself against liability to others

- Borrow money for the estate, with or without security, to be repaid from the estate's assets

- Advance money to protect the estate

- Arrange compromises with any person to whom the estate owes money

- Pay taxes, assessments and other expenses

- Sell stock rights

- Employ people

- Consent to the reorganization, merger or liquidation of a business

- Sell, mortgage or lease property in the estate

- Go to court to protect the estate from the claims of others

- Continue as an unincorporated business

- Incorporate any business

- Distribute the assets of the estate

Executor/Executrix/Trustee liability

An Executor/Executrix/Trustee may be subject to legal liability for various reasons such as the following:

- **Delaying the estate's distribution.** An Executor/Executrix/Trustee often is entitled to a year of grace, called the "executor's year," during which he or she manages the estate's interests, and the

note There are generally no set deadlines for the estate to be settled.

beneficiaries cannot bring him or her to court for not adequately fulfilling his or her responsibilities. Even after the initial year, the Executor/Executrix/ Trustee must blatantly neglect his or her duties for legal action to occur.

- **Wills variation law.** An Executor/Executrix/Trustee must wait for the will to be granted Letters Probate before he or she acts. Provincial wills variation legislation sets this time aside for the surviving spouse and children to petition the courts to have the will changed. When the Executor/Executrix/Trustee acts too soon, he or she may be liable.

- **Common-law relationships.** Most provincial laws stipulate that a common-law spouse of the deceased is entitled to a specific time period after the Grant of Letters to Probate in which to submit an application to the court for a share of the estate. This application is usually for ongoing support if he or she was a dependent of the deceased. Therefore, the Executor/Executrix/Trustee should postpone distributing the estate until after this time elapses when a common-law spouse is involved.

- **Revenue Canada.** The Income Tax Act stipulates that the Executor/Executrix/Trustee must obtain clearance certificates from Revenue Canada stating that all taxes, interest and penalties have been paid before distributing the estate. If the Executor/Executrix/ Trustee distributes the estate before clearance from Revenue Canada, by law, he or she will be liable for any unpaid taxes, interest, and penalties of the estate.

- **Beneficiaries' release.** He or she should have the beneficiary release him or her from liability (for adequately performing the job of Executor/Executrix/Trustee) by asking each beneficiary to approve and review the amount of the gift to be received. This signed document relinquishes any further claims against the estate by the beneficiaries, and avoids any personal liability to the Executor/Executrix/ Trustee for the amount of the gift.

- **Responsibility to act in good faith.** The Executor/ Executrix/ Trustee must act honestly, and without fraud or prejudice in conducting his or duties.

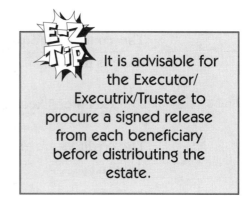

It is advisable for the Executor/ Executrix/Trustee to procure a signed release from each beneficiary before distributing the estate.

Probate

Upon your death, depending on your assets, your will may be submitted to the court by your Executor/Executrix/Trustee. The court determines that signatures are genuine, that you were free from delusions when you made the will, and that you were not pressured, threatened or tricked into making it, or forced to alter any of the terms of the will.

Definition:

Probate is the process by which the court gives its official approval to your will and by which your Executor/Executrix/Trustee is officially appointed.

If the estate is small or the assets of the estate are of a certain type probate may not be necessary. In this case, the Executor/Executrix/Trustee may be able to distribute the assets by making copies of the will for the designated beneficiaries.

Probate generally involves ten steps (not necessarily in this order):

A formal petition to admit the will to probate is filed with the court.

All interested parties are given notice.

If there is a will, the will is recognized by the court as genuine.

Unless waived, the Executor/Executrix/Trustee posts bond if the Executor/Executrix/Trustee is from outside the province.

The court issued probate. Letters of administration are issued when there is no will.

The Executor/Executrix/Trustee files an inventory with the court.

The creditors are given notice of time allotted to present claims against the estate.

All taxes, debts, and expenses of the estate are paid.

Beneficiaries receive their distributions after all limitation periods on claims to the estate are passed.

The Executor/Executrix/Trustee files a final account with the court.

The process of probate is necessary to protect both your wishes and your beneficiaries. One of the most important functions of probate is to make sure that the document you are submitting as your Last Will and Testament really is your last one. The court has to be sure that there is no other will that you wrote to replace the one submitted to the court.

HOT spot Remember, a will can be changed at any time up to your death.

Once your Last Will & Testament has been accepted by the court, the probate process ensures that your beneficiaries receive their inheritances exactly as you instructed.

Your personal inventory

For your Executor/Executrix/Trustee to administer your estate properly, at the time of your death he or she must have all the important information concerning your estate. This includes:

- a complete list of all of your assets. Include all of your real estate, the names of any co-owners and the location of any deeds. List all of your personal property and remember to write the replacement cost of each item—that is, what it would cost to replace the item in today's economy, not the price you originally paid for it

- copies of all group and individual insurance policies

- your vital records. Include your birth certificate, last will, marriage licenses and divorce decrees

- your cemetery plot deed and burial instructions or requests

- all retirement, pension or employee benefit plans with specific death benefits, including military records

- an inventory of all legal documents concerning your assets and liabilities, including any business agreements, partnerships, stockholder agreements, trust agreements or wills under which you are a beneficiary, pre-nuptial agreements, spouse's will, bonds, stocks, bank accounts, mortgages and any valuable special collections that you may have

- your tax returns for the past three years, including any gift tax returns

- a complete list of all of your debts and obligations, including any pledged assets, mortgages, personal notes or margin accounts with stockbrokers

- any other records that would help establish the value of your estate or that would help in the transfer of property after your death

Keep all of this information together in an envelope clearly marked "Will." Make copies, and store one set with each copy of your will. You can ensure your privacy by distributing a copy of the Document Locator form to your Executor/Executrix/Trustee or lawyer, rather than providing all your personal records. This will enable him or her to collect the information needed to administer your estate after your death. As your circumstances change, review and revise this information, as well as your will, regularly. Replace out-of-date copies with current ones and alert anyone having copies to the changes you have made.

Naming a guardian for your children

E-Z TIP

If you have minor children or dependents, you should name a guardian to care for said children or dependents in the event you leave them without another parent.

Since a guardian takes the place of a parent, name an individual who can offer the best care for your children or dependents, which in most cases will be a close relative willing to accept the responsibility. Also, make sure your appointed guardian is willing to do so and is of the proper age to raise your children. As with your Executor/Executrix/Trustee you should name an alternate guardian if the primary guardian cannot serve.

Answer the following questions before choosing a guardian for your child(ren):

- Does the person want to be guardian for your child(ren)?

- Does the person agree with you philosophically?

- Would your child(ren) be happy living with that person?

- Will the person be capable of supporting the child(ren) until they are older, with his or her money or your money that is held in trust?

- Have you left enough money?

- Do you need life insurance to provide for the children?

- Have you and your spouse selected the guardian together?

When you select a guardian for your child(ren) in your will, it is merely a request and not legally binding. The reason? Children are not property and cannot be left to someone. The law tries to determine what is in the best interests of the child(ren). In fact, if they are old enough, the child(ren) are permitted to voice their opinions. However, if the guardian is willing and able to assume the responsibilities of raising your child(ren), the courts will generally abide by your wishes.

Preparing your will

Preparing your will

5

As your last will and testament is a vital document, carefully consider how you want it drafted. You have several options.

Who should draft your will?

In Canada, there are four basic ways to prepare a Last Will and Testament:

1) Solicitor:

- fees vary

- discuss fee before you meet

- has training and experience in will preparation, especially in relation to trusts set up for dependents

- has insurance that can protect testator's intentions in the event that an error is made

2) Trust Company:

- usually wants to be appointed executor

- charges fees to administer the will

3) Notary Public:

- not available in all jurisdictions

- may lack experience in will preparation

4) Prepare your own will:

- save costly legal fees

- convenient and time-saving

- easy to complete by filling in the blank forms

- no recourse for beneficiaries if an error is made in the drafting of the will

It is not necessary to be a citizen of Canada to prepare a will. You should make the will in the province where you presently reside, although wills made elsewhere are also valid. Your estate is divided into assets that are moveable (such as furnishings) and immovable (land). Residence is important as it governs the jurisdiction over moveable assets. Immovable assets are always governed by the law of the province or jurisdiction in which the immovable property is located. Consequently, if you have land in another province, your will must be valid in that province. For example, if you have a holographic will, live in Alberta but have land in British Columbia, your will would be valid in Alberta in respect to your moveable and immovable assets in that province, but it would be ineffective in British Columbia in respect to the land you own there.

If married, both you and your spouse should prepare separate wills. This is true even if marital assets are primarily in the name of one spouse. If you have married, separated or been divorced after preparing a will, that will may now be invalid—be sure to discuss this with a lawyer.

In the course of making your will and planning your estate, you must choose your domicile—your legal residence. If you live in more than one province, your legal residence is usually the province in which you pay taxes, register to vote, and have registered and titled your car.

In all common law provinces, the spouse, children, and in some provinces, other dependents of the deceased are entitled to petition the courts for a larger share of the estate where the will does not provide adequately for them. The court has the authority to alter the disposition of the estate to provide for them. If you have remarried and have children from a prior relationship this can be especially relevant to your situation—be sure to discuss this with a lawyer.

If you have a dependent with special needs, you may wish to set up a "discretionary trust" for that dependent. Be sure to discuss this type of trust with a lawyer before you proceed.

Elements of a valid will

There are three elements the court looks for when it determines if a will is valid:

1) The will must be in writing. Although some provinces recognize an oral will, they do so under very limited conditions. An oral will that is made by soldiers in the military is an example of one such condition. Every province recognizes a written will.

2) The will must be signed by the testator. The testator can direct another to sign for him providing that the person signs the will in the testator's presence. You do not have to know how to write your name in order to sign your will, because the law will accept any mark that you want to use as your signature. Where special circumstances exist in relation to the testator signing the will, there are special attestation clauses that must be used in the will. Most provincial laws require that the testator sign at the end of the will.

3) The will must be attested to.
This simply means that there must be
at least two adult witnesses, who will
not benefit from your estate, willing to
sign your will. These witnesses must
be of sound mind and must sign after

the testator, in the presence of the testator, and each other. They must also
include their addresses. Be absolutely sure that your witnesses will receive no
inheritance from your will and that they are not your Executor/Executrix/
Trustee, an appointed guardian, your spouse, or any other relative. Your
witnesses must be of legal age and understand what it is they are signing, and
they must live locally in case a question should arise concerning the validity
of the will.

When is it necessary to prepare a new will?

Once prepared, your will is valid until revoked which may occur in one
of three ways:

- by cancellation or destruction

- by making a new will

- by operation of law, such as marriage

Other than under one of these circumstances, your will remains valid for
an unlimited time period. You can draft an entirely new will or add a codicil
(amendment)—do not write over the original or alter it in any way. This
invalidates the entire will.

A new will may be changed whenever you feel it is necessary. However,
you should prepare a new will under any of the following circumstances:

- **Change in financial condition:** A significant change in financial condition may necessitate a new will, as you may want to distribute your assets differently. You should also review your will when you acquire real estate in another province or country. Your will, to be effective in relation to real estate in another province or country, must conform to the laws of that province or country. In some situations it is beneficial to have two or more wills concurrently where you have assets in different jurisdictions. In this case you should consult with a lawyer. If you change your life insurance program, you should also review your will. If you have received an inheritance from parents, siblings, aunts, uncles or other relatives or friends, you should also review your will. If and when you acquire stocks or otherwise add to your portfolio, prepare a new will to designate to whom you wish to leave these new assets. When you change jobs and increase your income, consider increasing an existing beneficiary's share or, perhaps, adding another beneficiary—which requires a new will. On the other hand, you may be retired and decide to take that overseas trip while you are still healthy. You dip into your assets and now have that much less to leave your beneficiaries. Account for that difference in a new will. There can be many reasons for a change in financial condition. Don't allow the provisions in your will to restrict your financial decisions.

> **HOT spot** Remember, a new will may be drafted at any time before your death provided you are still mentally sound.

- **Change in your property ownership:** When you inherit or purchase property, you may wish to modify your will if you have not specified specific property in your will. If you have specified specific property that you no longer own or that you have substituted for other property, you should modify your will to keep track of these changes. For example, suppose you sell your summer house which you have bequeathed to your daughter in your will. Or, you retire, sell the family home, and buy a smaller condominium. Both of these circumstances require a new will because of the change in your property ownership.

- **Change in inheritance or tax laws:** If this affects your estate, you should alter your will. Estate planning laws, such as income tax law, trust law, and succession law, are constantly being revised. Consult with your legal and/or financial profession to determine if your estate will be affected.

- **Change in your Executor/Executrix/Trustee or beneficiaries' status:** Your Executor/Executrix/Trustee or beneficiaries may become incompetent, die, or be unwilling to serve. For example, you have prepared a new will after your husband has died to allocate your assets to your surviving family members. You have chosen your daughter to be your Executrix because she lives nearby. You become involved with someone new, but do not marry. Your daughter decides that she cannot handle the responsibilities of an Executrix/Trustee, and advises you to appoint your new partner as your Executor/Trustee. In this case, prepare another new will to change your Executor/Executrix/Trustee. Also, you might consider bequeathing something to your new partner.

- **Family additions:** The birth of a child may necessitate a new will, as your existing will may not properly provide for this child. Do you want to add a guardian clause and/or include him or her as a beneficiary? You may also add other dependents such as an elderly parent, brother, sister, aunt, uncle, adopted child or even handicapped friend as beneficiaries.

- **Move out of the province:** Prepare a new will when you move to a new province or country, even if there are

> *note* A newly prepared will helps establish your new province as your legal domicile.

no other important personal or financial changes. You want your will administered in the province in which you presently reside, because wills are generally administered in the province in which they are made, and your will may not be valid in your new province.

- **Marriage:** A marriage will revoke prior wills, so it is necessary to prepare a new will upon or before marrying (if you name your future spouse in the new will). For example, suppose you are single and already possess a will. You get married, and die suddenly without preparing a new will. The law considers this dying intestate because your previous will was revoked upon marriage, and you did not create a new one naming your spouse.

- **Divorce:** Unlike marriage, a divorce does not automatically revoke prior wills. However, in most provinces, your former spouse will not continue as a named beneficiary. Those provisions in your will that provide any authority, property or assets to your ex-spouse are void. Your will treats your ex-spouse as if he or she was deceased. If you desire to maintain bequests made to a former spouse you must prepare a new will.

- **Separation:** You must prepare a new will in order to change your beneficiaries and property ownership. If you do not have a separation agreement or a new will, your old will naming your estranged spouse as your primary beneficiary remains in force. 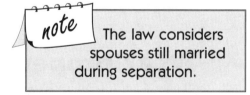 The law considers spouses still married during separation. Therefore, your ex-spouse will be entitled to a share of your estate should you die while you are separated.

These are only a few of many circumstances that would prompt you to revise your will. There may be many other situations, such as a child reaching adulthood, changes in personal relationships with family members or friends, or changes in health. For these reasons it is a good idea to review your will at least every year, so it is always up to date.

Never attempt to revise or change a will by altering an existing will. There are only two ways to revise an existing will:

1) **A codicil:** A codicil is an amendment to a will. It is recommended when you have only minor changes in mind. A codicil must be prepared, signed and witnessed in precisely the same manner as a will. When drafting the codicil, it is important to clearly state the changes so that there are no ambiguities or inconsistencies between the will and codicil.

2) **A new will:** A new will automatically revokes all prior wills and codicils. You should, nevertheless, revoke prior wills by formal cancellation so that your prior will is not mistakenly considered your most recent will. You can cancel a former will by actual destruction, or by writing across its face the words "revoked" or a similar term that clearly shows your intent to revoke it. Remember, you may not add words or provisions, or change, delete, strikeout or erase your will or codicil once prepared. You can, however, add more codicils.

A will is revoked with a revocation clause or by designating a different distribution of property in a later will or by marriage. It can also be revoked by cutting, burning, erasure or any other act that shows a clear intention to revoke the original will.

What property does not pass under a will?

A will does not dispose of property that would pass to another by contract or by operation of law. Common examples are:

- **Jointly owned property:** Where you own a home jointly with a spouse, for example, or have a joint bank account, or own stocks or bonds jointly, the jointly owned property will automatically pass to the other joint owner.

- **Property under contract:** If, for example, you had an agreement to sell your home and you died before conveyance, the buyer could nevertheless enforce the contract and the house would not become part of the estate, although the proceeds of the sale would.

- **Life insurance proceeds:** These funds are paid directly to the named beneficiary and do not pass under a will.

- **Living trust assets:** Property held in a living trust automatically bypasses probate. That is one reason why living trusts are so popular.

People often believe that once they leave property under a will they lose the right to sell or otherwise dispose of the property during their lifetime. This is not so. You fully retain the right to do whatever you choose with your property, notwithstanding its mention in your will. For example, the provision, *I leave to my brother Jack my 1990 Cadillac Sedan,* only means that your brother Jack inherits your 1990 Cadillac Sedan if you own it at the time of your death. If you traded the 1990 Cadillac for a 2000 Mercedes, your brother would not receive the Mercedes in its place.

Obviously, if your will includes many bequests that are no longer possible because you no longer have the items, it is time to prepare a new will to dispose of the assets you do have.

A look at your will

Examine the Last Will and Testament form in this guide. It contains the following elements:

The Opening Clause

The opening paragraph begins with the words "This is the Last Will of me,…." The purpose of this paragraph is to identify you as the person making the will, to identify your permanent address, to declare that you were of sound mind when the will was made, to declare this document to be your last will and testament, and to revoke and cancel any prior wills you might have made.

The Executor/Executrix/Trustee Clause

This paragraph begins with the words "I appoint…" This is where you name the Executor (if male) and Trustee or Executrix (if female) and Trustee whom you choose to administer or manage your estate after your death. The Executor and Trustee are the same person. Likewise, the Executrix and Trustee are the same person. Be sure to fill out the name of the alternate whom you have chosen as well.

The Administrative Clauses

This clause begins with "I give my…" and sets out the powers and restrictions to be placed on the Executor/Executrix/Trustee, in managing the assets of the estate and their distribution to beneficiaries.

The Bequests

Here is the main body of the will, beginning with the word "Bequests." (Sometimes, the term "legacies" or "devises" is used instead of the word "bequests"). This is the part of the will in which you leave the gifts to your beneficiaries. You name the specific person and the specific item that you are leaving that person. This is known as the dispositive clause in the will, because it is the place for you to dispose of your property.

Be sure that you, the testator, and your witnesses initial the bottom of each page. Notice that there is also a space for you to number each page. By filling in the page number at the bottom of each page and indicating the total number of pages in your will, you are preventing anyone from adding or deleting unauthorized pages.

The Debt Payment Clause

Beginning with the words "Debts to be Paid..." this clause lists the outstanding debts you wish to be paid out of your estate.

The Guardian Clause (optional)

If you have minor children, consider writing a guardian clause.

Beginning with the word "GUARDIAN," this clause names a guardian for your minor children. The guardian's role is to take care of your minor children in the event that neither of the natural parents are living.

Some of the duties of the guardian are:

- to possess and manage the minor's property

- to manage and invest the minor's assets

- to use the funds for the benefit of the minor

- to provide regular accounts to the probate court

- to file and pay the minor's taxes

- to distribute the remaining funds to the minor when he or she reaches adulthood

The trustee is the person who would be responsible for the maintenance of the estate for a minor beneficiary until that beneficiary is entitled to receive his or her full share of the estate. It is preferable that the trustee not be the guardian. Normally you do not want the guardian having the dual burden of raising the children and having to care for their money. There is also a good likelihood of conflict of interest in these situations. The guardian/trustee may decide that it is necessary for the transportation of the children that the guardian have a nice vehicle, like a Cadillac, paid for by the estate. It is usually recommended that you either choose someone other than the guardian to be in charge of the children's trust or that there be joint trustees, one of whom is the guardian.

You would usually appoint your spouse as guardian, but in the event that your spouse dies before you do or you both die at the same time, you need to appoint an alternate. It may not be a good idea to choose the child's grandparents if they are advanced in age. Since you want someone who can offer the best care for your child, a close relative who is willing to accept the responsibility is a good choice.

A sample guardian clause would read:

GUARDIAN: Should I die as the sole parent of any minor child(ren), I appoint _____ _____ as Guardian of said minor child(ren). If this named Guardian is unable or unwilling to serve, I appoint _____ as alternate Guardian.

Should you choose to insert this clause, be sure to re-number the clauses accordingly.

If the guardian is to be the guardian of the person and estate of the child, this should be clearly stated. The guardian's address should also be stated.

Where there is a trust set up for children, it is important to give some thought to when the child(ren) should receive their share of the estate. The point in drafting a will is to provide some personal directions in respect to your wishes that may not be reflected in prevailing legislation. For example, many parents are adamantly against leaving a 19 year old many thousands of dollars for fear they will not be able to handle such a large quantity of money in a mature fashion.

Normally, advances are paid when the child reaches the age of 19, 21, and maybe 25 with the remainder of that child's share paid when they reach 30. This requires proper trust provisions setting out that the trustee has discretion to use the income and capital of the gift for the child from time to time for educational, medical and other reasons that the trustee considers to be in the best interests of the child. In these cases, there also needs to be provision for payment of the funds to a guardian of the child as sufficient discharge of the trustee's liability. There needs to be some consideration with respect to the kind of investments that the trustee will be authorized to invest the money in through the life of the trust. There needs to be provision in the event the child does not live to be 30 but leaves a child or children of their own, or does not. In these cases, it may be best for the testator to see a lawyer.

The Residuary Clause

Beginning with the words "Residue of Estate:" this clause names the person who is to inherit the balance of your estate after all specific bequests have been distributed, and taxes and debts have been paid. In the event that this beneficiary fails to survive you by at least 30 days, his or her share will be divided equally between and among your surviving children.

The Signature Clause

Beginning with the words "IN WITNESS WHEREOF," this clause introduces the testator's signature. The testator's signature is his or her identifying mark, in place of the wax seal used a few centuries ago. The usual signature of the testator may be used even if it is not the same as the full name of the testator. On the other hand, it could be argued that if the testator signs the will in a manner that is not his usual signature, then the law

note The testator's signature establishes the end of the will and the date on which it was signed or completed.

has not strictly been adhered to. Therefore, however the testator signs his/her name, it must be his/her usual signature.

The Acknowledgment Clause

In the acknowledgment clause, the testator and witnesses sign their names in each other's presence and in the presence of the notary public. This is known also known as the "self-proving clause."

The acknowledgment clause acts as an affidavit, so that when a will is signed and notarized, the witnesses usually do not have to appear in court.

The Witnesses' Signatures

It is important that the witnesses not only sign their names, but provide their current addresses in case they have to be contacted. You will find that three signature lines are provided. Be sure to have at least two impartial witnesses sign your will.

Make certain your witnesses actually see you sign your will. Harvey, his witnesses, and the notary were gathered in Harvey's living room to sign his will. However, Harvey had failing eyesight and withdrew to the brightly lit kitchen to sign his will. Because neither the notary nor the witnesses actually saw Harvey hand sign the will, the court declared the will to be invalid. Similarly, if Harvey was in the same room as the witnesses but did not see the witnesses sign the will, the Courts have held such a will invalid.

Will provisions

Will provisions

Preparing your own will is not difficult. However, you must pay particular attention to the language you use to make your bequests. If you state in your will, *I leave my watch to my daughter,* you know which watch and which daughter you are referring to. Would this be clear to someone else? You may have the diamond-studded Rolex in mind for your bequest, but you have forgotten about the broken Timex you threw into your desk drawer two years ago when the battery ran down. To avoid any confusion, describe the exact watch and the specific daughter who is to receive it.

Avoid confusion

The language you use in your will establishes your intentions. The more specific the language, the clearer your language will be to others.

Be as precise as possible.

Do not use words such as "desire," "hope," "want," "pray," "would like," "believe," or "request" when making your bequests. These are not words of intent. They simply reflect your wishes.

Use as much detail when describing your property as is necessary to identify it.

Here is another example of a bequest that is too vague:

I give my collection of books to my sister Alice Smith.

Unless you want your sister to inherit every single book in your home, you have to be more specific. A clearer statement of your intentions may be:

I give my collection of 50 rare, leatherbound first editions located in the oak bookcase under the window in my study to my sister Alice Smith.

In this case, your sister would only inherit 50 valuable volumes.

When describing real property if you want to leave a specific property:

- List the addresses

- Describe the plot, parcel and the name of the development

Be careful when using words that indicate quantity. Words such as "all," "every," and "entire" mean that there are no exceptions. In addition, words such as "some," "few," and "several" have no precise meaning other than to indicate that you mean more than one. Try to describe the number of items whenever possible. When you mention your children, name each child to whom you are bequeathing property to. Do not use phrases such as "my children" unless you mean all of your children, including natural children, stepchildren and non-marital children.

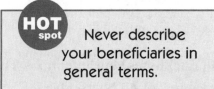

HOT spot — Never describe your beneficiaries in general terms.

Making special bequests

You will continue with special bequests, wherein you leave specific assets to certain beneficiaries. Consider this type of bequest carefully. Are there family heirlooms that would have special meaning to someone? Should you leave a war souvenir to an old army buddy? If you are a mother, wouldn't it make sense to leave your jewelry to your daughters? You see the idea. A special gift may not have monetary importance but may have personal significance. Bequests should always be clear, complete and specific as to who is to receive what property.

Examples:

I give my 1992 Chevrolet Caprice to my son Harry Smith.

or

*I bequeath to the Second Baptist Church of Center City
the sum of $10,000 to use in any manner the church deems proper.*

Your special bequest should also indicate whether the property is to be gifted subject to mortgages or encumbrances against it, or whether it is to be gifted free and clear, with any debts against the property paid from your general estate.

Examples:

*I leave to my daughter Mary Smith my home at 5 Maple Street,
Center City, subject to all mortgages.*

or

*I leave to my dear friend Harry Carlson my 1986 Chris Craft
Sedan Cruiser, free of all encumbrances.*

Debts

All debts of the deceased must be paid by the Executor/Executrix/ Trustee before distributing the assets of the estate to the beneficiaries. The Executor/Executrix/Trustee is also responsible for costs relating to probating the will, the funeral, and all legal fees before distributing the bequests under the will. The law establishes priorities if there are too few assets in the estate to cover such costs.

In the event that the assets do cover all these debts and expenses, but what remains is not enough to cover the specific bequests and gifts of money, those remaining assets are divided proportionately among the beneficiaries according to the specifics of the will.

Under a will you may release a person from obligation to repay money owed you. If a person you release from a debt is a beneficiary, you should state whether he is to receive his full bequest or whether the debt first is to be deducted.

Example:

I leave $100,000 to my nephew John Smith, less such balance on the $20,000 loan that he then owes me.

It is important to be clear on this point, particularly between parents and children. For example, if you gave your son $50,000 for a down payment on a home, was this a gift or a loan? If it was a loan, should it be deducted from whatever your son may receive under your will?

A *per capita bequest* leaves property distributed in equal shares to all entitled beneficiaries as in this example:

I leave all my property to my children who may survive me, in equal shares.

The key to this wording is the fact that each child receives an equal share. Simply divide the property by the number of children surviving you.

A *per stirpes bequest* divides property up in a more specific manner, such as:

I leave all my property in equal shares to my children, but if any child shall predecease me, I leave that child's share to his or her children.

Here, the grandchild or grandchildren can inherit only the proportion or amount that their parent was entitled to inherit. The children take the place of the parent and stand in his or her shoes for the purpose of inheritance. This is often called inheritance by rights of representation.

It is often wiser to choose a per capita bequest over a per stirpes bequest. For example, Sally bequeathed all of her property equally to her two sons, Charles and Harry, or their lineal descendants, per stirpes. Charles had one child and Harry had two children. Both Charles and Harry died before Sally. When Sally dies, Charles' child inherits one half of the estate while Harry's children must share their half. Therefore, Harry's children each receive one quarter of the estate. If Sally had left her estate per capita instead of per stirpes, each grandchild would have received one third of the estate.

Disinheritance provisions

In all provinces, it is extremely difficult to disinherit a child. If you wish to disinherit a child or other dependent, it is important that you specifically mention the child and your intention to disinherit. If you simply omit mention of a child, the law

You may wish to completely disinherit a child or spouse. Consult legal counsel if this is the case.

presumes you forgot the child and entitles the child to his or her moral and legal share. Proper language to disinherit may read, for example:

Since I have not heard from my son John Smith in more than five years, I leave him nothing.

Or

I recognize my daughter Mary Smith is financially secure, and therefore leave her nothing.

In some provinces, it is impossible to completely disinherit a spouse, as the spouse is entitled to at least some share. If it is your intention to disinherit your spouse but you are uncertain of the laws in your province, you may use this language as an example:

I leave to my wife, Ellen, absolutely nothing, or,
if unlawful to do so, such minimum share of my estate
as shall be required by law.

After six months, a spouse or dependent (including common-law spouses) may commence legal action when you don't bequeath adequate funds to him or her. The court often orders the costs of such litigation to be deducted from the estate. In addition, when you do not leave enough money for your spouse and dependents, your other beneficiaries will incur a decrease in their share of the estate by the amount you were originally supposed to give to your spouse and/or dependents as well as the legal costs resulting from the claim. Your other beneficiaries must wait until the conclusion of these court proceedings to collect.

> **HOT spot** Remember, it is often wise to leave your children and spouse some bequest so as to avoid a contest over your will.

Residuary bequests

The "residuary" clause names the "residuary beneficiary," the person or organization who will receive (other than specific bequests) the remainder of your estate. Because the residuary clause distributes your remaining property, it is often called your "safety net." It accounts for assets that might fall through the cracks in your will. If you have no residuary clause in your will, overlooked assets would be distributed as though you had no will. You may wish to avoid specific bequests altogether, in which case your will shall only contain a residuary bequest.

If your will contains no specific bequests, the residuary clause may read:

I leave all my property to my wife, Hilda Jones.

If there are specific bequests it would read:

I leave all the rest of my property to my wife, Hilda Jones.

Wills frequently state the residuary clause more completely as:

*I leave all the rest and residue of my estate, including both
real estate and personal property, and wheresoever located,
to my wife, Hilda Jones.*

Since it distributes any portion of your estate not accounted for by specific bequests, anything you have forgotten to include will be accounted for under your will. Suppose you forgot to include a valuable piece of jewelry or you came into possession of a valuable painting long after you had prepared your will. The residuary clause prevents those items from falling through the cracks in your will.

Alternate gift provision

It is possible that a named beneficiary may predecease you. Just as it is always wise to name an alternate Executor/Executrix/Trustee and alternate guardian for your minor children, it is wise to name an alternate for each beneficiary you list in your will. You might use a clause such as:

*I leave all my property to my wife Hilda Jones,
but if she shall predecease me, I leave said property to
The Second Baptist Church of Center City.*

Or

I leave all my property of every nature and description to my wife, Hilda, but if she shall not survive me, I leave said property to my surviving children in equal shares.

HOT spot Remember, if you name an alternate beneficiary for a child or other dependent, that alternate does not have to be another child or dependent.

Theoretically, there is no limit to how many levels of alternate beneficiaries you may name. Alternate beneficiaries may be effectively used to create different plans for distributing your estate. You may for example, feel obligated to leave everything to a specific person but in the event that person predeceases you, you may then feel free to make specific bequests to other relatives, close friends, or even to charities. Be sure to specify the share each of your beneficiaries is to receive.

It is also important to consider what should occur if you leave property to your children but a child dies before you do. Should that deceased child's share be distributed among your other children, or would you prefer that child's share to be distributed among his or her children (your grand-children)?

There is, of course, no one correct answer to this, but here are alternative ways of expressing your wishes:

I leave all my property to my children who may survive me, in equal shares.

Or

I leave all my property in equal shares to my children, but if any child shall predecease me, I leave that child's share to his [or her] children equally.

Other contingent bequests

Do not name your pet as a beneficiary. Animals are considered property, and one property cannot own another property. If you have strong feelings about providing for the future care of your pet, feel free to make outside arrangements, perhaps with a veterinarian. If you intend to leave your pet to a beneficiary as a gift, do not surprise that person with the pet. Get his or her permission first.

Do not include a body or organ bequest in your will. It is unlikely that your will can be read in time to allow for the donation. You should make separate arrangements for this type of donation. Even if you can make the donation, remember that medical schools do not accept every donated body, so be sure to make alternative arrangements in case yours is rejected.

Charitable donations

Be sure that the particular charity to which you wish to leave money has been approved as "charitable" by tax authorities. If so, that donation could be credited towards the assessment of federal taxes on your estate. Make sure you have the correct legal name of the charity so the right charity receives your donation.

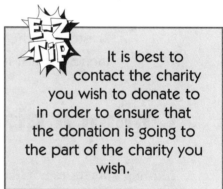

It is best to contact the charity you wish to donate to in order to ensure that the donation is going to the part of the charity you wish.

Passing on your business

If you own your own business, you must consider what will happen to your business if you suddenly pass away or become disabled. Among other things, include clauses in your will to assign your immediate replacement.

Whether you want the business to be sold or not, you still need someone to manage it in the interim. You may appoint your spouse, one of your employees or your Executor/Executrix/Trustee.

Include a clause in your will outlining a short-term emergency arrangement for your business. Consider the following factors:

- If you are training your children to run the business, and they are prepared to immediately replace you upon your death, bequeath the business to them.

- If your children are not prepared to step in now but will be capable soon, you may bequeath your business to them with the provision that your Executor/Executrix/Trustee manage the business or employ someone to manage the business until they are completely capable.

- If there is no one in your family who can competently manage your business at any time, provide in your will for the sale of your business. However, contemplate having your Executor/Executrix/Trustee run the business until it is sold. He or she may obtain more money for it if it is still operating when it is sold.

Common disaster clause

Although one does not like to think about it, you must consider what happens to your estate if both you and your spouse or even your entire family perishes at the same time. You may add a survivorship clause explaining how you want your estate distributed should this occur.

Unless you state to the contrary, your estate's distribution depends upon who died last. If you died last, the estate would go to your family. If your spouse died last, it would be distributed to her family. To prevent one side of the family from receiving the entire estate, you may each include a clause in your respective wills that should there be a common disaster the estate is to be equally divided between both sides of the family. This negates the need to probate the same assets twice.

Otherwise, you may stipulate in your wills that a beneficiary must outlive you by a specific amount of time, i.e., 30 days, before he or she is entitled to obtain any share of the estate. Such language eliminates the need to probate the estate twice.

Adopted children clause

Most provinces treat adopted children as though they were the parents' natural children. However, different provinces use different words to describe children: "issues," "heirs," "descendants" or "children." If you include a clause in your will that clearly defines what you want the word "children" to mean, the possibility of any confusion can be avoided later on. Such a clause might read:

By the use of the word 'child' or 'children' in this will,
I mean any and all children lawfully adopted by me
at any time before or after the making of this will.

Stepchildren, unless legally adopted by the non-biological parent, only have rights to their biological parent's estate under intestate law. Likewise, children born out of wedlock may only inherit from a biological parent. A child born through artificial insemination inherits from the husband of the birth mother, not from the semen donor, and a child born from a surrogate mother has no rights to the estate of the surrogate mother but does have rights to his/her legal parents' estate.

Cemetery bequest clause

While you may direct that all funeral expenses be paid from your estate, it is not a good idea to include specific funeral arrangements in your will, because the funeral may be over before the will is found. Specific arrangements may be included as per a separate document or part of your Statement of Wishes. However, it is not uncommon to make a special bequest to a cemetery for the perpetual care of a cemetery plot. These arrangements—in fact, all funeral arrangements—should be made in advance so that you can bequeath the appropriate amount of money.

A sample clause may read:

> *I bequeath $5,000 to Mary Knoll Cemetery for the*
> *perpetual care of my cemetery plot.*

Funeral expense clause

It is usually the responsibility of the Executor/Executrix/Trustee to see that funeral expenses are paid out of the money in the estate, but some provinces make the surviving spouse responsible for those expenses. It is a good idea to include a clause directing where the money to pay the funeral expenses is to come from. A sample clause may read:

> *My debts and expenses of my funeral and burial*
> *shall be paid out of my estate.*

Incorporation by reference clause

To incorporate a separate document into your will, you must make reference to it in your will with this clause. A sample clause may read:

> *I hereby intend to, and do, incorporate by reference into this will*
> *the following document dated January 1, 1998, which is now in existence*
> *at the time of this writing and is located at 500 Main Street, Anytown, PA.*
> *The document is described as follows: A listing of individual paintings*
> *and the intended beneficiary of each painting.*

You may only incorporate a document into a will by reference if that document actually exists at the time the will is executed. Documents cannot be incorporated into the will as they come into existence, if at all, at some future time.

Pour-over clause

Even people who choose to avoid the time and cost of probate by putting all their assets in a living trust should have a will, if for no other reason than to insert a pour-over clause into it. A pour-over clause states that any asset inadvertently left out of a trust should, at the time of death, be automatically added to that trust.

For example, John Smith purchases a valuable coin for his collection and plans to do the paperwork necessary to transfer it to his living trust. But he is killed in an auto accident before he can do so. Can the coin still be placed in the living trust? Yes, through the use of a pour-over clause in John's will. This clause states that items outside of the living trust "pour over," or are automatically added to the trust upon the testator's death. A sample pour-over clause in John's will might read:

The remainder of my estate, wherever located, I bequeath to the trustee or trustees named under a certain revocable living trust executed by me on January 1, 1995, between myself and the trustee of the John Smith Trust in the county of Any county and the province of Any Province, to be added to the principal of the trust and to be administered in all respects as an integral part of that trust.

Savings clause

In the event that any of the clauses in your will are found to be invalid, you do not want the entire will to be revoked. A savings clause accomplishes exactly that: it saves the will. A sample savings clause might read:

In case any of the separate provisions in this will are found to be invalid, the invalidity of such a provision shall not affect the validity of any other provisions in this will, since it is my intention that each of the separate provisions shall be independent of each other, allowing all valid provisions to be enforced regardless of the validity of any of the others.

What cannot be done in a will

One of the basic principles that govern all wills is the idea of lawfulness. If it was illegal during your lifetime, you cannot use your will to make it legal.

You cannot use your will to libel or defame another person. If you write a false statement about another person, and it becomes a matter of public record, as a will does, your estate may be liable for damages. Do not try to damage another person's reputation through your will.

You cannot require someone to commit an act that is illegal in order for that person to inherit under your will. A will cannot be used to violate public policy or command something be done that is not in the person's best interests.

Planning your funeral

7

Planning your funeral

7

Thinking about your own funeral may be an unpleasant thought. However, death is a reality that must be faced. Important decisions must be made and responsibilities must be confronted. Make it easier on the loved ones you leave behind by discussing your wishes with them and planning beforehand. Take practical steps, and your loved ones will be consoled by knowing they respected your wishes and beliefs.

First, you may not even want a funeral. However, consider its purpose. The funeral provides a chance for your friends, family and anyone who knew you to share in their love and grief. The funeral often serves the religious, social and psychological needs of your survivors and also brings comfort to them when they can mourn collectively.

Your funeral services

Should you decide upon a funeral, pre-arrange your funeral with the funeral director. Discuss the type of service you want, music, clergy, casket and final disposition of your remains. Notify your family, friends and your physician when you have decided upon an appropriate funeral home, and finalized arrangements.

note A respectable funeral home will help you in completing pre-arrangement forms.

Pre-arrangement can be accomplished by:

- Paying the funeral home in advance

- Paying the funeral home in installments

- Writing instructions to your next of kin regarding your wishes

- Putting aside money at a bank for the occasion

- Indicating whether you want your estate or next of kin to pay the costs

Advantages of a pre-arranged funeral

In addition to saving your family money, the following are advantages of a pre-arranged funeral:

- **Eases the responsibilities of your survivors.** By taking care of your funeral and cemetery arrangements beforehand, your family, friends and Executor/Executrix/Trustee do not have to make the decisions.

- **Your decisions are meaningful.** Since you have thought carefully about what you want when you are well, your decisions are rational and reflect your wishes. Such decisions include whether you want a traditional or simple funeral, and your wish to be cremated, buried, or interred in a mausoleum.

- **Shields you from inflation.** When you pre-pay, your money is held in a trust account which earns interest and is legislated by provincial law. Money must be returned to the estate if funeral costs

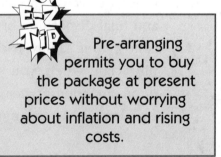

Pre-arranging permits you to buy the package at present prices without worrying about inflation and rising costs.

are less than the funds held in trust. You also relieve your family of the financial burden of a funeral.

- **You may shop around.** Without pre-arrangement, your family may not have time to compare prices, services, and facilities of different funeral homes.

When pre-arranging a funeral, you sign an agreement. But ask the following questions before signing:

- Are you entitled to a refund if you change your mind?

- Are you entitled to a partial refund if you want to be cremated or have a memorial service instead of a regular funeral?

- Does the provincial law for that funeral home permit them to hold back a portion of the funds paid as a fee in the event you cancel? If so, how much?

- What is their policy if you move from the area?

- What happens if they go out of business?

- Can you cancel the contract 30 days after signing and get a full refund?

Laws vary from province to province regarding rights of cancellation and refunds. Check your provincial regulations. Depending upon the province, some funeral homes are not affiliated with cemeteries and crematoriums, so you may have to make special arrangements to buy a burial plot or be cremated.

Memorial donations

People often express their sympathy by making donations in the deceased's name. You may designate a particular charity or cause for this purpose. Choose one you have a sincere interest in. Perhaps, you would like to establish a memorial fund for educational purposes. In any case, your survivors should be tactful with these requests. They do not want to appear as though they are soliciting money. A funeral director can help with the language of the request.

Legal documents

The funeral director will acquire and fill out the necessary forms to facilitate the process of recording your death with the appropriate departments. He or she will also complete the forms for cremation and/or burial. The forms and language may differ from province to province. However, the following comprise the common documents required:

- Funeral director's Statement of Death

- Provincial government Death Registration Form

- Medical Certificate of Death from the doctor, or Medical Certificate of Death from the medical examiner when the death was investigated by the Office of the Medical Examiner

- Burial Permit

- Cremation Authorization

- Out-of-province Transportation Authorization

Choose a funeral provider

A funeral provider must be licensed to own and conduct business. "Full-service" providers possess their own premises for services. "Satellite" funeral providers work in conjunction with full-service funeral homes.

When you select a funeral home, consider the following:

- How long has it been in business?

- Are you aware of its reputation?

- Does the funeral home and funeral director possess a local and provincial license to operate?

- Does it belong to the provincial Funeral Service Association?

- Is it a full-service funeral home large enough to satisfy your needs?

- Does the funeral home have a chapel, visitation room, reception area, and provincially licensed personnel?

- Does it belong to the Better Business Bureau? Have there been any complaints?

- Do you know anyone who has used it?

- If you desire a recommendation, will the funeral director provide you with references?

Memorial societies

Join a memorial society when you do not want to shop for funeral homes. Membership entitles you to a fixed-price funeral. The memorial society negotiates the price with a specific funeral home.

The service

You can choose from several types of funeral services:

The traditional funeral service

The traditional funeral service includes a ceremony conducted in a church or funeral home while the body is there. Burial or cremation follows the service. After consulting with the family, the funeral director or member of the clergy directs the service. Family members or friends often deliver eulogies. The service may include special music, songs, poems, or literary passages that epitomized the deceased. The survivors may or may not want the casket open for viewing. The decision depends on personal and religious preferences and circumstances. The traditional funeral service requires the use of the funeral home's personnel, premises and equipment for three to four days for:

- Moving the body from the place of death

- Filing and obtaining the required government documents and permits

- Arranging for special services

- Embalming and dressing the body

- Supplying the casket and limousines

- Furnishing the flowers and acknowledgement cards

- Immediate disposition. Immediate disposition involves:

- Transporting the body from the location of death

- Putting the deceased in a casket or other container

- Securing registration of death and burial permit

- Obtaining other required documents

- Supplying a funeral director's Statement of Death

- Obtaining a casket

- Using premises

The Executor/Executrix/Trustee is responsible for the charges for transporting the body to the cemetery and/or crematorium.

Fraternal or military services

Any past or present member of Canada's military has rights to military honours. This involves covering the casket with the Canadian flag, and having a bugler perform taps. Such organizations as the Royal Canadian Legion and Army, Navy and Comrades-in-Arms may supply pallbearers and an honour guard, if so desired. Ask the funeral director to get in touch with these organizations to procure the appropriate people. Some cemeteries contain a Field of Honour and Cross of Sacrifice. Past or present members of the military must request permission to be buried there.

Memorial service

Like a traditional funeral service, a memorial service can be conducted in a church or funeral home and can be any size. However, the body is not present in a memorial service. They are usually held instead of a funeral when the death happened overseas, the body was cremated or the body is unavailable.

> *note* Because the body is not present, a memorial service can be conducted anywhere including the family home or outdoors.

Financial assistance

Financial assistance for funeral costs is available through a number of sources. If you have been a contributor to the Canada Pension Plan, your estate will qualify for aid. If you were a veteran, Veteran's Affairs Canada provides benefits. When the death was related to work, Workers' Compensation provides financial help. Consult your company, union, association or fraternal group to inquire about death benefits. Life and accidental death insurance provide stipends to cover funeral costs should you have such a policy in force.

Instructions for completing your will

Instructions for completing your will

These instructions will guide you in filling in the blanks of the will provided with this manual.

❶ Type or print your name on the center top line so the will is identified as yours

❷ Restate your name

❸ Enter the street address where you reside

❹ Enter the city where you reside

❺ Enter the province where you reside, if applicable. This is where your will may be probated

❻ Enter the number of the day

❼ Enter the month

❽ Enter the year

❾ Identify whom you wish to appoint as your Executor/Trustee or Executrix/Trustee

10 Enter the city of your Executor/Trustee or Executrix/Trustee.

11 Enter the province of your Executor/Trustee or Executrix/ Trustee

12 Enter the name of your Executor/Trustee or Executrix/Trustee

13 Enter the name of alternate Executor/Trustee or Executrix/ Trustee, should your first named Executor/Trustee or Executrix/ Trustee be unable or unwilling to serve

14 Enter the street address of alternate Executor/Trustee or Executrix/Trustee

15 Enter the city of alternate Executor/Trustee or Executrix/ Trustee

16 Enter the province of alternate Executor/Trustee or Executrix/ Trustee

17 List your special bequests. Note that the sample will only contains two special bequests, but you may have many such bequests

18 Number each page: i.e. page one of two, page three of eight

19 Testator initials here

20 1st witness initials here

21 2nd witness initials here

22 List outstanding debts you wish your estate to pay

23 Enter the name of the person(s) to receive the rest of your estate after the specific bequests have been distributed and debts paid

24 Enter appropriate pronoun

㉕ Enter the name of the person(s) to receive the rest of your estate after the specific bequests have been distributed and debts paid

㉖ Enter the number of preceding pages

㉗ Enter the city in which you are signing this will

㉘ Enter the province in which you are signing this will

㉙ Enter the number of the day

㉚ Enter the month

㉛ Enter the year

㉜ Sign your will exactly as your name first appears. Be sure you sign in the presence of your witnesses

㉝ Enter the name of the testator

㉞ Each witness should sign his or her full name and complete address. Make certain your witnesses are disinterested parties and sign in each other's presence after the testator signs and in the presence of the testator

㉟ Testator initials here

㊱ 1st witness initials here

㊲ 2nd witness initials here

Bear in mind that your will may contain other types of provisions. You may, for example, desire to have property held in trust for a beneficiary. These and other possible

note File a *Wills Notice* with the appropriate government agency if applicable in your province.

provisions should be carefully considered before drafting your will. Don't forget: schedule a review of your will each year so it remains up-to-date.

Signing your will

Read your will carefully to ensure that it accurately reflects your intentions. The will must be signed by you in the presence of at least two independent witnesses. The witnesses cannot be:

- persons who are or may become entitled to receive any benefit under your will (i.e., your beneficiaries)

- your spouse

- your Executor/Executrix/Trustee

Once your witnesses are present, sign the will on the last page where indicated and make sure that the correct date appears on the will above your signature. All other pages of the will (excluding the last page) must be initialed by you in the bottom right hand corner of each page.

Each witness must sign the last page of the will where indicated, then they must print their full names, addresses and occupations. Each witness must also initial each page of the will (excluding the last page) at the bottom of each page specified "Witness' Initials."

To ensure the validity of your will it is important to have it properly witnessed. While the law requires two witnesses only, it may nevertheless be a good idea to use three (3) witnesses in the event a witness becomes disqualified. If a witness is also a beneficiary under the will, the witness is not disqualified, only the gift is void. The rest of the will is retained.

Witnesses must be disinterested parties and therefore cannot be named in the will as a beneficiary, Executor/Executrix/Trustee, or guardian. Never allow a relative or spouse to sign as a witness. Witnesses should also be of age and reside locally, in the event a question should arise concerning the validity of the will.

Safekeeping your will

Sign the will and then make copies of the original. Never keep the original will in your home. If your home burns down and both you and the will are destroyed, you may not have a will. It is best to keep the original will in a safe-deposit box. Make certain that one or two family members know of its location. If you are in a province with a Wills Registry, such as British Columbia, make sure you file a Wills Notice with the province so that your will is easy to find and there is some proof that no subsequent wills have been made.

Another copy should be left with whomever you designate as Executor/Executrix/Trustee of your estate. Yet another copy should be retained by your attorney.

Living
Will

What is a living will?

What is a living will?

Today, medical science is capable of extending the lives of terminally ill and comatose patients longer than ever before. These patients who once died quickly from their inability to eat or drink, sometimes suffer unbearable pain. Because modern medicine can now cope with these problems, every patient, while still in good health, has the opportunity to decide exactly which life-prolonging medical procedures he or she does or does not want to be used during his/her final days.

Common Names

These decisions are made through a living will, sometimes called:

- an advanced directive

- a personal directive

- a representation agreement

- a healthcare directive

- a mandate

- a directive

- an authorization

A living will has different names depending upon the province in which it is written and/or used. Sometimes a living will not only expresses your wishes concerning continued medical treatment when you cannot consciously do so, but it also may appoint someone to make health care decisions for you.

However, it is recommended that you use a separate document called a *Power of Attorney for Personal Care* to designate the individual whom you want to carry out the instructions contained in your *Living Will*.

The living will applies only to comatose patients who can no longer communicate their wishes to terminate life-support systems. In a living will, a person conveys his wishes with respect to being kept alive indefinitely by employing life-extending procedures or artificial life support systems (life-prolonging treatments) when becoming fatally ill or critically injured. The living will informs your family, friends, and doctors about your feelings regarding life-prolonging treatments. It eliminates the need for your family to make a painful life or death decision about your extended medical treatment when you become incapable or can no longer communicate.

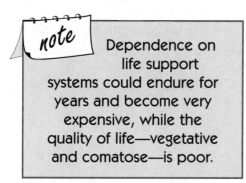

note

Dependence on life support systems could endure for years and become very expensive, while the quality of life—vegetative and comatose—is poor.

Your living will removes the guesswork about your intentions when you become terminally ill, and provides peace of mind to family members, spouses and friends and whomever you designate as your attorney for personal care. It allows you the choice of a natural death in lieu of being hooked up to a machine such as a respirator without hope of being revived.

What do you want your attorney for personal care to do if you are terminally ill? End-of-life treatment instructions are generally contained in your living will. Provide him or her:

- Broad instructions depending on level of consciousness, extent of pain and suffering, odds of living, or other quality of life elements

- A detailed list of treatment choices according to your specific condition

While the idea of surrendering to death, or the right-to-die, may be frightening no matter how peaceful or natural, it is preferable to suffering a meaningless and prolonged artificial existence. The decision to surrender to a natural death has come to be known as the "right-to-die." The living will is often called a "right to die" or "death-with-dignity" form. Many legal scholars, religious figures, and physicians now acknowledge that a person is entitled to die a natural death. Anyone who desires to save his or her family the torment and exorbitant cost of extended care for the terminally ill, suffering patient should make a living will.

> **HINT** If you favor a dignified death to a life sustained by respirators, feeding tubes, and dangerous drugs, make a living will.

The will is called a living will because, unlike testamentary wills (last wills) that take effect after you die, the living will takes effect before death. It differs from a Last Will and Testament which states how property is divided after an individual's death. In any case, do not wait until you are ill and incapable to sign a living will.

Healthcare providers

Healthcare providers are frequently reluctant to honor the requests of seriously ill patients because they cannot be certain that the decisions were rationally made. A living will expresses, while rational, your intentions to your physician when you cannot make your preferences known.

In the past, death was a private matter that took place in your home with your family present. Now, it is more likely that your death will occur in a hospital or nursing home. Therefore, it becomes more important than ever to have legal protection from unwanted life-prolonging procedures should you become ill.

Your power of attorney for personal care

10

Your power of attorney for personal care

10

In addition to having a living will, you should also create a power of attorney for personal care. It is a legal document which is utilized to designate someone to act or make decisions for you when you become incapacitated—a substitute decision maker. The power of attorney for personal care extends beyond your incapacity. You should always make the wishes regarding life sustaining procedures expressed in the living will uniform with those in your power of attorney for personal care.

Choosing your power of attorney for personal care

Choosing your substitute decision maker is one of the most important decisions you will ever make. It is literally putting your life in someone else's hands. Think carefully about whom you can trust with your life because your decision maker will have many duties including life and death decisions.

Most provinces allow you to select an individual to make healthcare and/or personal decisions for you when you become incapacitated. This person may be called:

- a health care proxy

- representative

- substitute decision maker

- a power of attorney for personal care

- an agent for personal care

By appointing a power of attorney for personal care you ensure that your welfare becomes the responsibility of someone you know and who knows you—not a government official. You should also appoint an alternate power of attorney for personal care. The attorney for personal care should be:

- **Someone you trust.** Trust is one of the primary factors in choosing your attorney for personal care. You will be unable to personally monitor his or her actions and decisions. You must be certain of his or her ability to handle life and death situations. You also must be certain that he or she cares about you enough to act in your best interests instead of what is best for him or herself. You must be confident that he or she can act quickly in emergencies.

> **HOT spot** Remember, the attorney for personal care will be responsible for your medical care when you are incapacitated.

    This person must be able to comprehend medical information received from physicians or healthcare practitioners. He or she must weigh the benefits and risks of proposed treatment, and make a decision based on what you would want for yourself, not what he or she would want for you. He or she must be able to deal with doctors and other professionals, and not be afraid to ask questions.

- **Someone who comprehends your personal philosophy about death.** Your decision maker must be someone who understands how you feel about prolonging life by artificial means, how you wish to live, and how and when you wish to die. He or she must be acquainted with your beliefs and values. It might even help to discuss your religious beliefs with your decision maker in order for him or her to fully understand the "whys" of your feelings. This way he or she can carry out your wishes, and be confident that he or she has acted properly.

- **Someone who will faithfully follow the instructions contained in your living will.** You must choose someone who is devoted to you, and can understand and carry out the living will's instructions no matter what the circumstance. For example, suppose you have chosen your daughter as your substitute decision maker. You stipulate that you wish to live in a nursing home should you become incapable. A nursing home would be expensive, and perhaps dip into her inheritance. She might feel that she could care for you better. However, you feel that while you have the money you don't want to be a burden to anyone. She must comply with you living will's instructions even if it is not emotionally and financially advantageous to her.

- **Someone who will enforce your rights as a patient.** Voluntary passive euthanasia, or dying a natural death without prolonged medical treatment that would artificially extend your life but not cure you, is your right as a patient. A living will authorizes that choice.

note It is your substitute decision maker's duty to carry out the wishes contained in your living will.

- **Someone who is mentally competent.** A substitute decision maker must be able to think and act quickly. He or she must understand the options available to you, and make a decision. He or she must be able to act under pressure and handle stress.

- **Someone who can understand the ramifications of treatment choices.** A substitute decision maker must be able to anticipate the effects of further medical treatment. He or she must decide when to deny life prolonging treatment if you have expressed your wishes to refuse it in your living will. The attorney for personal care must weigh the benefits against the risks of further treatment when specific instructions for that treatment are not included in your living will. He or she must consider the resulting quality of life, chance for recovery, chance for survival, pain factor and what he or she thinks you would want to do in that particular situation based on his or her acquaintance with you.

- **Someone who can live with his or her decisions.** When you have expressed your wishes through your living will or discussed them with your substitute decision maker, your substitute decision maker does not have to make his or her own decision. However, if you do not have a living will, have not discussed your wishes with your substitute decision maker or have suddenly become incapacitated, someone must make the decisions about your medical treatment. Therefore, choose a strong individual who will use his or her best judgment and be able to live with his or her decision—without guilt or remorse.

- **Someone who is younger than you.** Preferable choices for the position of attorney for personal care include a spouse, adult child, close friend, relative, religious and legal advisor, business partner, life partner, companion, or other trusted individual. However, do not choose a trust company. While they may handle estates, they are not legally permitted to be attorneys for personal care.

    The attorney for personal care must be someone who is immediately available in an emergency. Hopefully,

E-Z TIP Designate an alternate decision-maker who lives nearby just in case the long-distance one cannot be immediately reached.

this person would either live with you or in the vicinity. You may choose a person who lives in another city or province—or even country—with the confidence that he or she can be reached when needed via modern communications such as cell phones.

Discuss your living will's instructions and personal feelings about prolonged medical treatment with your attorney for personal care as well as with your whole family. This ensures that the decision-maker will have the full support of your other relatives in his or her capacity as your attorney for personal care. And, needless to say, make sure the person you appoint is willing to serve in that capacity.

In some provinces, a public official often known as a public guardian, takes care of the personal matters of incompetent adults when commanded by the courts. The public guardian may work out of the public trustee's office (in Ontario and Manitoba), or he or she may be part of a separate department (in Alberta, Prince Edward Island, and the Northwest Territories). If you do not have a power of attorney for personal care, and no one is available to obtain a court order for a guardian who is acquainted with you, you may come under the jurisdiction of one of these public officials. In addition, even if you name a public guardian as your attorney for personal care, he or she may or may not want to serve in that capacity. Therefore, if you choose this option, check with the public guardian beforehand. Contact your local public trustee to inquire whether there is a public guardian in your province, and how to locate him or her.

Duties of an Agent for Personal Care

In your power of attorney for personal care, you may have special requirements for your decision-maker to ensure that he or she acts responsibly. You may require him or her to report to select individuals, keeping them apprised of your condition. This becomes helpful if the family does not live nearby and/or does not get along. For example, suppose you are put on a respirator. You live in Ontario with your spouse who is your attorney for personal care. Your brother lives in Newfoundland, but your spouse and brother do not talk. Wouldn't you want

to be certain that your brother is informed about your situation? Give explicit instructions in writing, however difficult that may be when you are of sound mind and in good health.

You might also stipulate that he or she maintains a record of decisions made—to be reviewed by another individual. For example, you designated your spouse as your attorney for personal care, but you have a son-in-law who is a doctor. You might want your son-in-law to be consulted before any major medical decisions are made.

In addition, consider having your mental competency tested from time to time to make sure you cannot make your own decisions before the services of an attorney for personal care are required. Designate a family doctor, home care nurse, psychologist or social worker to evaluate your mental state. A signed and dated statement by the designated person will attest to the fact that you are mentally incompetent, and, once attached to the power of attorney for personal care, the living will will come into effect. For example, the law in Alberta specifically provides for the designation of someone in your power of attorney for personal care to evaluate your mental state *before* a substitute decision maker may be consulted.

Women might consider adding a clause to give instructions about what should be done in case of incapacity while pregnant. This is essential if you live in Prince Edward Island as the law in that province prohibits decisions regarding abortion unless the mother's life is in jeopardy. In these times, it is not uncommon for a woman to have a baby without having a mate. You may be settled in your career and financially independent, but have not found that special someone. You may be pregnant, and become incapable with no one to care for the child. Under those circumstances, should you desire an abortion, you may use a power of attorney for personal care to state so.

If you have appointed more than one substitute decision maker, you also should include a proviso dictating how disputes should be settled should a disagreement arise between the two decision-makers. Suppose you have appointed your two children to act jointly as substitute decision makers. You have been declared incompetent because you are comatose. The doctor informs your two children that the only way to keep you alive is to insert a feeding tube. You did not complete a living will because you could not confront these end-of-life choices. Instead, you left the decision to your substitute decision makers in your power of attorney for personal care. Your son insists that you would want to be kept alive. Your daughter disagrees. However, they must act jointly in arriving at a decision. Suggest in your power of attorney for personal care that they both submit to mediation rather than going to court. It is a cheaper, friendlier, and more efficient means of resolving disputes.

In general, the duties of an attorney for personal care are to:

- **Select the most comfortable, and least painful course of action available.** This may involve refusal to consent to a feeding tube, consent to administration of pain killers for a terminally ill cancer patient, a do not resuscitate order for a heart patient, etc.

- **Act honestly and in good faith.** The appointed decision maker must be forthright in dealing with doctors and other healthcare professionals. He or she must carry out the wishes expressed in the living will and if those wishes are not expressed, he or she must act faithfully in accordance with what he or she thinks those wishes would be. He or she must base his actions on his or

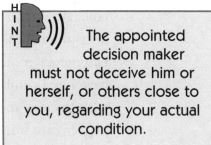

HINT The appointed decision maker must not deceive him or herself, or others close to you, regarding your actual condition.

her understanding of you and your principles. He or she must not act according to what he or she would do in your situation, but must instead consider what you would want for yourself. A substitute decision maker must not be selfish. For example, suppose you appointed your son to be your attorney for personal care. You have told him in these discussions that you want to die peacefully and naturally. Your son, on the other hand, believes that "where there is life there is hope." He wants to keep you alive under any circumstances because he loves you very much, and can't face your death. And, it goes against his principles. In this case, your son cannot be selfish and act upon his wishes and beliefs. As an attorney for personal care, he must act according to your wishes, as conveyed during your discussions with him. He must put your wishes before his.

- **Communicate with other family members, especially long distance ones, and close friends.** Nowadays, this becomes especially important as it is common for families to be geographically spread apart. In times of emergency, family members and friends are concerned and deserve courtesy phone calls. Doctors first inform the substitute decision maker about the patient's condition. Therefore, it is his or her responsibility to keep your friends and family up-to-date on your condition. He or she could utilize a system whereby he or she calls one individual and asks him or her to call other persons on your "list." You might even include this list as part of your estate planning documents.

- **Get necessary medical treatment for you.** Should you suddenly collapse in your home or otherwise become gravely ill, it is your decision maker's duty to contact your doctors, and/or get you to an emergency room as soon as possible to obtain treatment. Once you have been admitted to a hospital, your decision maker must consult with doctors about your condition and ensure that you receive the proper care from nurses, and any other healthcare professional that treats you. Your decision maker must be aware of any medications you are allergic to as well as the medication you take. You should provide your decision maker with this list of medications once he or she accepts his or her role.

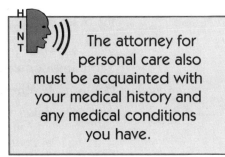

The attorney for personal care also must be acquainted with your medical history and any medical conditions you have.

- **Follow admissions and discharge procedures from an institution.** Should a healthcare practitioner recommend hospice

note The decision maker must do what is necessary if you require a nursing home.

for your final days, the decision maker must sign the appropriate documents for discharge from the hospital and transfer to the hospice facility. Should you recover from your illness, and be discharged from the hospital to go home, your decision maker must be your liaison with the hospital and guide you through the discharge process.

- **Examine medical records and agree for them to be disclosed to others.** Often, physicians want to see your other doctors' medical records. As medical records are generally confidential, it is the decision maker's responsibility to ensure your records are handled correctly, and that they reach the appropriate people.

- **Sign necessary documents from and for healthcare providers regarding medical treatment.** Hospitals and physicians must document their actions in writing. Likewise, a decision maker must sign papers to either consent to or refuse to consent to life-prolonging treatment.

- **Decide upon living arrangements, including where and with whom.** When you are released from a hospital because nothing more can be done to improve your condition, an attorney for personal care must decide where you are to live (if you have not addressed this issue in your living will). It can be in his or her home, a nursing home, hospice, a child's or spouse's home, a life partner's home, a brother's or sister's home or any other place that the decision maker deems workable and appropriate.

- **Confer on legal matters that involve you such as personal injury claims.** If you were involved in a car crash that caused incapacity or death, and the other party files suit against you or vice versa, your attorney for personal care must be consulted about the case as he or she is privy to your medical information.

- **Release from liability those who act upon the decision-maker's orders.** Most provinces provide for this through laws governing power of attorneys for personal care. These laws specifically require as inherent in the document itself, the release of physicians and hospitals from liability when they act upon the decision maker's orders. This prevents lawsuits or criminal allegations of voluntary active euthanasia when the substitute decision maker refuses life-prolonging treatment.

- **Ensure the validity of your living will in any province that it is used.** Before you create a living will, consult the laws of your province. You should also review your living will when you move to another province. In the event you have done neither or there are no laws governing the creation of a living will, a living will still provides guidance to healthcare practitioners, your family and your attorney for personal care. It is your attorney for personal care's responsibility to provide the living will to healthcare practitioners, and urge compliance with it even where there are no such laws in that province.

- **Hire or fire individuals to care for you, such as home-care professionals, nurses, etc.** If you are released from a hospital to your home, and still are incapable, your decision maker becomes responsible for employing home-care professionals, nurses and other healthcare practitioners to take care of you. He or she must monitor their work to ensure you receive the best care possible, and, if you do not, he or she must terminate them and find suitable replacements.

By clearly stating your end of life instructions, the job of your attorney for personal care will be that much easier. If, for some reason, you cannot focus upon end-of-life treatment in your living will, have your substitute decision maker decide upon the best course of action based on his or her acquaintance with your values and beliefs.

When you don't have a power of attorney for personal care

If you have not appointed an attorney for personal care, or that individual refuses to, or cannot act, you will not have someone to make decisions for you if, or when you become incapacitated. In both cases, the province will locate a substitute decision maker for you. The public official will first ask one of your family members to either grant or withhold consent for further medical treatment.

Your spouse will be the first family member to be approached. If you are not married, your adult child will be asked. If you do not have adult children, the next in line is a parent. If both parents are deceased or unavailable, an adult brother or sister is consulted. If you have no siblings, the province will contact your closest linear adult relative.

However, if the provincial official cannot locate your closest adult relative, and you don't have any relatives willing to assume the responsibility, the physician and/or hospital will contact the public trustee or public trustee and guardian of the province. This person will make the final decision for you.

Even if you do not have a power of attorney for personal care, any person who consents or withholds treatment for you is supposed to follow the instructions contained in your living will. If the particular situation is not addressed in your living will, that individual must consider whether further treatment will improve your quality of life and/or the risk factors involved.

note

Healthcare facilities, long-term care residencies, and nursing homes, for example, are leaning towards requiring power of attorneys for personal care, even if a family member can technically step in without one.

Immediate family members may be permitted to make health care decisions on your behalf if you do not have a power of attorney for personal care. Close family members may get involved especially in medical emergencies.

To ensure that all your wishes regarding healthcare are executed upon becoming terminally ill or incapacitated, you should create both a living will and a power of attorney for personal care.

Euthanasia

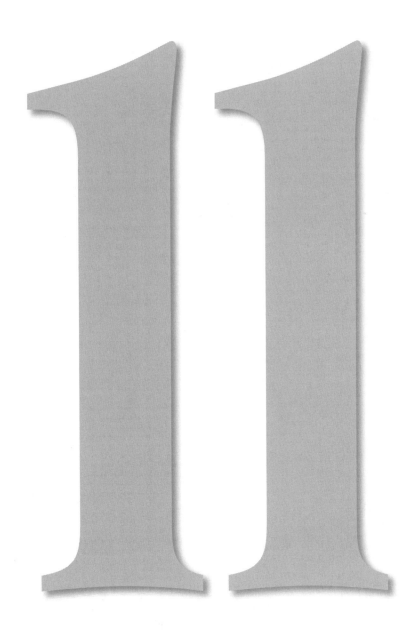

Euthanasia

Euthanasia literally means "good death," and for that reason is often used interchangeably with the term "death with dignity." You should be familiar with the different types of euthanasia. There is only one which is allowed by the law and sanctioned by a living will.

Voluntary passive euthanasia

This is the only type of euthanasia authorized by a living will. These are simply instructions to your physician not to undertake medical acts necessary to prolong your life when death would naturally occur in the absence of such treatment. In some provinces this may include the use of intravenous feeding but it universally will include such procedures as the use of respirators. It always requires the consent of the patient.

Voluntary active euthanasia

This type of euthanasia is never authorized by a living will because—not withstanding the fact that it may be merciful—it may be viewed as homicide even though the patient consents to it. In fact, the doctor can

> **note** Voluntary active euthanasia requires that the physician take positive or active steps to end the patient's life.

be charged under the Criminal Code. Administering a drug overdose or lethal injection to a terminally ill cancer patient, or providing the patient with medications with which to end his own life are examples of voluntary active euthanasia. This practice is commonly called "doctor assisted suicide." A physician is never required to follow these instructions when contained in a living will.

Involuntary passive euthanasia

This refers to the withholding of medical treatment without the patient's consent. This is never authorized by a living will, and also may be viewed as homicide. If the patient is unable to give his or her consent to the withholding of medical treatment, then it is the substitute decision maker's responsibility to give or refuse consent to further medical treatment.

Involuntary active euthanasia

This too may be merciful, but since the patient's life is actively terminated without his consent, it too will certainly be viewed as homicide. A substitute decision maker cannot force a healthcare practitioner to perform such an act.

Withholding food and fluids

Most terminally ill patients feel little hunger and experience a gradual decrease in thirst. This may be due to disease which often causes extreme pain or nausea. As a result, patients often stop eating and drinking completely. This is a natural part of dying and many believe does not

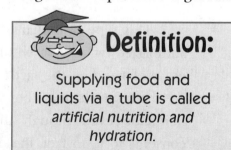

Definition:

Supplying food and liquids via a tube is called *artificial nutrition and hydration.*

increase the patient's discomfort. The Courts believe that artificial hydration is one of those medical procedures that a terminally ill patient has the right to refuse. You should stipulate in your living will whether you want to undergo artificial nutrition and hydration and under what circumstances. It is up to your substitute decision maker to carry out your wishes.

The validity of living wills

Any competent adult can execute a living will. In some provinces the minimum age to prepare a living will is 16 while in others it is 18 or 19. You must also be mentally sound. Evidence of mental illness or ongoing psychiatric care does not automatically prevent you from preparing a living will and simple absent-mindedness or forgetfulness is not evidence of mental illness. But should you have a history of serious mental disorders, consult with a qualified medical practitioner just prior to preparing your living will. This will help establish your competency.

Whether or not your procince or territory has yet passed legislation regarding directives, it is still a good idea to have a living will because healthcare practitioners must follow your clear instructions when known.

Of course, a parent can always decide that extraordinary medical procedures should not be used to prolong a child's life, nullifying the need for a living will. Conversely, if the child wants to die but the parents insist on prolonged efforts, the wishes of the parents will prevail.

A foreign citizen can make a living will that will be valid in Canada. Such a living will shall be honored to the same extent as a living will prepared by a Canadian citizen. If the individual prepared a living will in a foreign country, it will be recognized to the same extent a living will prepared in another province would be recognized.

Provincial
laws

Provincial laws

12

As previously mentioned, laws regarding living wills and powers of attorneys for personal care vary from province to province. These documents may have different names depending upon the province in which you reside.

> **note**
>
> There have not been any serious legal disputes regarding the validity of living wills and powers of attorney for personal care.

Be aware that even if a law has been passed by the legislature, it does not yet mean that it is in effect. An act must be "proclaimed in force" in order for it to be fully enforceable. Some provincial laws have been passed, but have not yet been "proclaimed in force" such as in British Columbia. Except for Quebec, these advance directive laws are comparatively recent—the oldest one was passed in 1988 while the majority of them have passed since 1992.

The different provincial laws vary in their complexity. Some simply permit a living will and power of attorney for personal care to be written, while others explicitly monitor the activities of decision makers and/or necessitate the registration of the documents with government offices. These advance directive laws also vary regarding the age at which these documents can be drafted—some laws are based upon age while others are based upon the individual's capacity to understand the concept and scope of these documents. However, all of the laws provide people, while they are still able, with the means to appoint a decision-maker and to convey their instructions regarding end-of-life treatment and personal care.

Review the laws for your province from the section below before completing your living will and power of attorney for personal care. Become familiar with the rules and regulations governing these documents.

British Columbia

Under The Representation Agreement Act, 1996, any adult who is at least 19 years old can provide instructions regarding health care, personal care, or financial affairs with a "representation agreement." It must be in writing, signed, and witnessed.

In this province, the decision maker is referred to as a "representative." He or she can be an adult or the Public Trustee. The law provides the representative with the authority to make basic decisions regarding the following:

- personal care such as where to live

- entrance to a healthcare facility

- management of business affairs

- management of healthcare

- management of legal affairs excluding divorce

Any of the foregoing powers may be excluded from your representation agreement.

The act also provides for optional decision making authority, such as:

- allowance to restrain, move, or manage you even if you object

- agreeing to healthcare even if you object

- disallowance of specific kinds of healthcare including life support

- arranging for the care of your children

- managing your business

- investing money

The law stipulates one tier of mental capacity that is necessary for you to create an agreement designating the basic decision making powers, and another level for creating an agreement containing the optional decision making powers. You are allowed to make an agreement containing the basic provisions even if you are unable to make a contract or handle personal, healthcare, legal, business, or financial affairs. On the other hand, you can empower your representative to make the optional decisions only if you are mentally competent—that is, you comprehend the nature and effect of the authority you are giving.

If you designate more than one representative:

1) state their respective areas of responsibility

2) designate one of them as your principal representative to act as spokesperson

3) explain a system for resolving disputes among them

You may designate an alternative representative, but you must specify when he or she should act and under what conditions. In addition, when creating your representation agreement, decide whether you want another person to monitor or supervise your representative.

You must register your representation agreement with the Office of the Public Trustee of British Columbia in order for it to be effective. Nevertheless, a representative can effect his or her powers upon an unregistered agreement when:

- your best interests must be protected

- you have signed your agreement

- you have sent or are about to send your agreement for registration

- your representative informs the registrar that he or she has acted or will act

- your agreement authorizes action

The Act specifies the responsibilities and authority of representatives as follows:

- they must act in good faith

- they must, if possible, confer with you to understand your wishes

- they must act upon your values and beliefs to the best of their knowledge

- if your values and beliefs are unknown, they must act in your best interest

Representatives are entitled to the information required to make decisions and are obligated to maintain the confidentiality of that information. The appointed monitor must ensure that the representative performs his or her responsibilities, and is permitted to speak to him or her at any time. If the monitor discovers that the representative is acting improperly or not acting at all, the monitor must take the initiative to ensure compliance even if it entails notifying the Public Trustee. The Representation Agreement Act contains provisions for the ousting of a representative and/or monitor as well as for the cancellation of the agreement. The Public Trustee of British Columbia also has the authority to conduct an investigation into the representative's actions should anyone register a complaint.

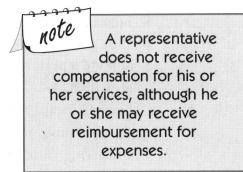

note A representative does not receive compensation for his or her services, although he or she may receive reimbursement for expenses.

Alberta

In 1996, the legislature of Alberta passed the Personal Directives Act which states that any individual who is at least 18 years old and comprehends the nature and effect of a directive may write one or more of them. It must be dated, witnessed, signed and in writing. In this province, the individual selected to be the decision maker is referred to as an "agent." The agent and the agent's spouse are not allowed to act as witnesses.

The directive may include information and directions about any personal issue such as:

- healthcare

- living quarters

- persons with whom to live and associate

- schooling, work and social activities

- legal concerns

The directive may also include directions to:

- appoint an agent and specify his or her powers

- indicate those individuals who are banned from acting as agent

- appoint a person to evaluate your condition, and establish the point at which incapacity exists. A directive takes effect when you become incapacitated. The individual selected in your directive for this purpose must confirm your incapacity in writing after conferring with a doctor or psychologist. If you have not assigned anyone for that purpose or that person is unavailable, a declaration of incapacity is signed by two healthcare providers ("service providers"), one of whom must be a doctor or psychologist.

- designate those persons who are, and who are not, to be informed when the directive becomes effective

- instruct about obtaining confidential information

A directive may not contain instructions to perform any illegal actions. Under the law, such instructions are void.

The agent's responsibilities include:

- conferring with you before he or she makes a decision

- making decisions according to your directions in the directive

- recording his or her decisions

An agent is not permitted to make decisions about the following treatments unless the directive expressly orders the agent to do so:

- psychosurgery

- sterilization that is not medically necessary

- extraction of tissue for transplanting or research

Healthcare providers (or service providers) also have the responsibility to:

- Make a prudent effort to locate your agent, and if he or she cannot be found, attempt to contact your closest relatives to apprise them of the situation.

- abide by your agent's directions

- always ascertain whether you are incapacitated before providing further treatment

- inform your agent if you have recovered from incapacity

- confirm your agent's identity and powers

You can rescind your directive at any time provided you are capable. In addition, there are three conditions that terminate a directive:

1) if you recover from incapacity

2) death

3) court order

An agent receives compensation for his or her services only if your directive provides for it. Otherwise, payment is not allowed. However, your agent and/or his or her spouse are still entitled to inheritances as beneficiaries if named in your will, life insurance, pension, etc.

A directive protects agents and service providers from liability for their actions if performed in good faith. However, it is against the law for long term health care facilities such as nursing homes to require a directive in order for you to obtain or keep your housing.

Saskatchewan

The legislature in Saskatchewan passed the Health Care Directives and Substitute Health Care Decision Makers Act in 1997. The law provides that any individual at least 16 years old who is capable of making health care decisions may have an advance healthcare directive. This healthcare directive shall take effect when that individual loses his or her capacity. The healthcare directive must be in writing, dated, and signed.

In this province, the decision maker is called a "proxy." The proxy must act in accordance with your wishes. If you have not discussed your wishes with your proxy, he or she must make decisions based upon your best interests. If you do not have a directive, do not choose a proxy, or if your proxy cannot act, then your relatives have the authority to make healthcare decisions for you. Your proxy or relative is entitled to obtain the necessary confidential information to arrive at a decision.

Manitoba

In Manitoba, the Health Care Directives Act, passed in 1992, declares that any individual who is able to make healthcare decisions can have a health care directive. The act implies that persons at least 16 years old are capable. Any individual who has a health care directive is assumed to be at least 16 unless there is evidence to the contrary.

Under this law, a directive must be dated, signed, and in writing. The directive takes effect when you become incapable of making decisions yourself or you cannot communicate. Divorce automatically terminates a directive.

The appointed decision maker is referred to as a "proxy." He or she must be a minimum of 18 years old and must perform his or her duties guided by the following precepts:

- follow the instructions in the directive

- abide by your wishes, if known

- act in your best interests

A proxy is not permitted to make decisions regarding the following unless so stated in the directive:

- medical treatment for research purposes

- sterilization that is not required for the preservation of your health

- extraction of tissue for transplanting or research

The Health Care Directives Act contains provisions regulating decision making if you appoint more than one proxy, and they disagree. The court is permitted to evaluate the proxy's conduct and dismiss or replace him or her.

A proxy is entitled to confidential medical information and is shielded from liability for actions performed in good faith. A proxy is still entitled to his or her rights under a will or other document.

Ontario

The individual who is responsible for making healthcare decisions for you if you are deemed incapable is called:

- a substitute decision maker

- an attorney for personal care

- a representative

A healthcare professional who suggests treatment must first assess whether a person is capable. An individual is deemed capable if he or she is able to understand the relevant information for making a decision about the treatment, and able to understand the consequences of that decision. This includes data regarding

note In Ontario, The Health Care Consent Act governs the procedures which caregivers must follow for obtaining consent from their patients for medical treatment.

the treatment's nature, benefits, risks, side effects, and other available options to the treatment. The individual must also be able to understand the results of not having the treatment. A patient is assumed capable unless he or she seems disoriented or afflicted. A health practitioner is not permitted to believe an individual is incapable due to age, disability or a psychiatric or neurological condition. If the individual is capable, the practitioner obtains an informed consent and performs the treatment. If the individual is not capable, the doctor must advise the patient that a substitute decision maker will be privy to discussions and have the ultimate authority to make a final decision as to whether or not to continue treatment. If the incapable individual disagrees with the determination of his or her incapacity, he or she may ask the Consent and Capacity Board to review the incapacity finding. Likewise, if the individual objects to the involvement of a substitute decision maker, he or she may request another substitute decision maker.

When a substitute decision maker must be consulted, he or she is defined according to the Health Care Consent Act in the following order as:

1) the individual's guardian, if the guardian has the power to agree to or deny treatment

2) the individual's attorney for personal care as designated in a power of attorney for personal care if such power of attorney for personal care grants power to make that particular decision

3) the individual's representative selected by the Consent and Capacity Board

4) the individual's spouse or partner

5) the individual's child (over 16 years old) or parent or a children's aid society or any other person who has the right to give or deny consent to the treatment instead of the parent

6) the individual's sibling

7) an individual's closest relative

8) the Public Guardian or Trustee when none of the above can be reached

The Act stipulates that a substitute decision maker must be at least 16 years old and must make his or her decisions according to the individual's desires if they were conveyed while he or she was capable. If the substitute decision maker is not acquainted with the person's wishes, he or she must base his or her decision on the individual's best interests. Best interests means whether or not the considered treatment will improve, prevent from degenerating, or lessen the degree of the degeneration of the incapable patient's condition.

If a doctor or healthcare practitioner who suggests a treatment feels that the substitute decision maker did not consider the incapacitated person's wishes or best interests in making his or her decision regarding the proposed treatment, the doctor or healthcare practitioner may petition the Board for a ruling regarding whether the substitute decision maker complied with the Act's requirements. If the substitute decision maker did not meet the requirements, the Board may force the substitute decision maker to make decisions based upon the incapable individual's best interests.

The law permits substitute decision makers to make the decision to admit incapacitated persons to care facilities for purposes beside further treatment such as shelter or personal assistance services. Personal assistance services mean assistance with routine activities of daily living such as hygiene, dressing, grooming and eating.

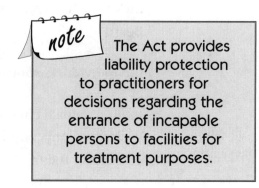

note

The Act provides liability protection to practitioners for decisions regarding the entrance of incapable persons to facilities for treatment purposes.

Patients who have been declared incapable and have a substitute decision maker requested for them have specific rights under the Act such as the right to:

- apply to the Consent and Capacity Board for a review of the incapacity declaration

- ask for a different substitute decision maker of the same or higher level

- ask the Consent and Capacity Board to appoint a different representative

- provide a power of attorney for personal care to someone else

A power of attorney ends when:

- the attorney dies, becomes incapacitated, or quits

- the court appoints a guardian

- the individual makes a new power of attorney document

- the power of attorney for personal care is revoked

Quebec

The Quebec Civil Code contains a "mandate" law providing for the creation of a mandate, otherwise known as a contract or agreement, which permits an individual referred to as a "mandator" to assign a "mandatary" to make medical decisions for him or her. Literally, the document is called "an agreement of mandate", although the English translation for it is "power of attorney."

According to the law, the purpose of the mandate is to ensure the protection of the mandator in case of his or her incapacity. The "personal mandatary" makes decisions regarding his or her health. Anyone at least 18 years of age can make a mandate. It must be in writing and notarized or else signed by two witnesses. In order for it to become effective it must be confirmed or "homologated" by the court.

If a mandator recovers from incapacity, the mandate's effects terminate. This is assessed by court order or by a document filed with the clerk of the court from the department head of the institution supplying treatment to the mandator. The mandatary may not cancel his or her appointment by the mandator unless he or she names a successor or has provided for institutional supervision for the mandator. The mandatary must act wisely and avoid a conflict of interest with the mandator.

Nova Scotia

The Medical Consent Act states that any individual who is at least 19 years old and capable of agreeing to medical treatment can empower someone to consent for him or her, if she or he becomes incapacitated. This delegation must be in writing, signed, and witnessed by anybody besides the appointed decision maker or his or her spouse.

Unlike other provinces, the decision maker does not have a special title, but is considered to be a "guardian." The authorization terminates when:

- the author revokes it

- a court order appoints a guardian

- a judge revokes it by order

An application can be submitted to a judge to:

- revoke the authorization

- replace the existing decision maker with someone else

- for other relief

Prince Edward Island

According to the Consent to Treatment and Health Care Directives Act, 1996, anyone at least 16 years old may have a directive. The directive must be signed, dated, and in writing. In this province, the decision maker is called a "proxy." In order for the selection of the proxy to be enforceable, the proxy must consent to his or her appointment in writing before the patient becomes incapacitated.

The directive applies to the following:

- authorization for medical treatment

- dying a natural death with only care to alleviate suffering

- selection of a proxy

- point at which directive takes effect

- instructions for healthcare or treatment

A doctor may prescribe medicine for pain relief regardless of the directive's instructions. On the other hand, a health practitioner who wants to treat an incapacitated patient is permitted to receive consent from the following in order:

1) proxy

2) guardian

3) Spouse

4) child or parent

5) brother or sister

6) close friend

7) relative

If after exhausting the above list, no one is available or if there is a conflict among those consulted, the public officer who has the authority of the Public Guardian makes the decision.

Decisions regarding the following are prohibited:

- medical research that is not useful to the patient

- sterilization that is not necessary

- abortion unless the life of the mother is in jeopardy

- electric shock used for behavior modification

- extraction of tissue for transplantation

Practitioners must make a reasonable effort to find out whether a patient has a directive. Directives must be registered, and once registered, they are considered enforceable. The law provides for revocation of a directive as well as an evaluation of the proxy's behavior by the Public Guardian or other public official. A patient may not be deemed incapable because he or she does not have a directive.

A proxy is guided by the following tenets:

1) Follow the directive's instructions, or if not available, follow the person's known desires.

2) Make sure that any wishes conveyed after the directive's signing are carried out.

3) Act in the person's best interests even if wishes are unknown.

4) Have the person participate in the decision if at all possible.

The proxy must consider the person's "best interests" which considers:

- the individual's philosophy

- the individual's present desires, if communicable

- whether the proposed treatment will help the individual's condition

- whether the individual's condition would deteriorate without the proposed treatment

- whether the advantages out number the disadvantages

- whether a different treatment would be as effective.

A proxy has the right to access all the essential information before he or she gives his or her consent.

Newfoundland

The Advance Health Care Directives Act, 1995, states that a capable individual has the right to create an advance healthcare directive that provides treatment instructions or specifies his or her values regarding the type of treatment he or she wants. The directive must be in writing, signed, and witnessed by two people.

The individual also has the prerogative to select a substitute decision maker to act on his or her behalf when he or she becomes incapacitated. The substitute decision maker must be at least 19 years old and must acknowledge the assignment in writing.

The directive takes effect when the individual becomes incapable of conveying and formulating decisions. It remains in force while the patient is incapable.

Unless specifically stated, the substitute decision maker does not have the authority to agree to the following:

- treatment for research

- unnecessary sterilization

- extraction of body tissue for transplants or scientific research

The law assumes that a directive was made just prior to the loss of capacity, and that a person must be at least 16 years old to be able to make a directive. Divorce automatically terminates the appointment of a spouse as a substitute decision maker.

The law also provides for an order of eligible substitute decision makers when an individual has not appointed one and does not have a guardian. The following people, in descending order, must have had personal contact with the patient within the preceding 12 months of the incapacity:

1) spouse

2) children

3) parents

4) siblings

5) grandchildren

6) grandparents

7) uncles and aunts

8) nieces and nephews

9) other relative

10) healthcare practitioner

Northwest Territories

Presently, no laws are in effect regarding directives in this province. An individual may still have a directive describing his or her choices for healthcare treatment as the general law directs healthcare providers to abide by your wishes. However, without an advance directive law, no legal method exists for choosing a substitute decision maker. In addition, if someone disagrees with your wishes, there is no assurance that they will be followed.

Yukon

Presently, no laws are in effect regarding directives in this province. An individual may still have a directive describing his or her choices for healthcare treatment as the general law directs healthcare providers to abide by your wishes. However, without an advance directive law, no legal method exists for choosing a substitute decision maker. In addition, if someone disagrees with your wishes, there is no assurance that they will be followed.

New Brunswick

Presently, no laws are in effect regarding directives in this province. An individual may still have a directive describing his or her choices for healthcare treatment as the general law directs healthcare providers to abide by your wishes. However, without an advance directive law, no legal method exists for choosing a substitute decision maker. In addition, if someone disagrees with your wishes, there is no assurance that they will be followed.

In general, provincial laws for living wills and power of attorneys are still evolving. Law makers are trying to:

- Provide the patient the right to make his or her own medical decisions.

- Provide the individual the option of selecting someone to make decisions for him or her.

- Provide those substitute decision makers with the legal power to abide by the individual's instructions.

- Provide a legal system that protects the individual, the medical practitioners, and government officials (if they become involved) from burdensome red tape or high administrative expenses.

Moving to another province

If the new province recognizes living wills and powers of attorney for personal care it will generally honor a living will and power of attorney for personal care prepared in another province. If the new province does not recognize living wills and powers of attorney for personal care, it may or may not choose to recognize your living will.

However, as provincial laws vary, it is a good idea to review your living will and power of attorney for personal care when you move to another province. This ensures that the language of your estate planning documents as well as the legal requirements regarding age, witnesses, etc. conform to local laws.

Preparing your living will

13

Preparing your living will

This guide contains a standard living will. It may be completed, signed, and witnessed. You also have the option to change the stated guidelines for terminating treatment or to add other specific directions not included in the original form. For example, under what circumstances do you request termination of treatment? Do you want food and water artificially administered or discontinued?

Be specific with your instructions. For example, you might not want to be hooked up to a machine. However, respirators that assist in breathing are often employed on a temporary basis during emergency surgery. That is a different situation than being dependent on them to stay alive.

Define the situation. Provide the appropriate instructions for the physical or mental condition you are suffering from depending upon whether it is permanent. Consider whether you desire specific treatments for specific situations.

Consider the varying degrees of the illness. For example, a stroke might be mild or severe. Your instructions for treatment would be different if your stroke was mild and your chances for a higher quality of life were greater. Also, be aware of directions regarding medication.

Types of medical treatment

It is possible to state more precisely the medical treatment you want to refuse and, conversely, the medical treatment you would accept. Some examples of the type of treatment you can accept or reject include:

- cardiopulmonary resuscitation (CPR)

- mechanical breathing (respiration)

- artificial nutrition and hydration

- major surgery

- kidney dialysis

- chemotherapy

- invasive diagnostic tests

It is not absolutely necessary to specifically define these points within your living will, but you should consider them and discuss them fully with your family and physician so those people can more fully share your feelings.

Witnesses for your living will

E-Z TIP

After you have signed your living will, you should have two witnesses sign your living will in your presence and in the presence of each other.

Never have anyone whose interests may be in conflict with your continued existence witness your living will. This would include anyone who is an Executor/Executrix/Trustee or beneficiary under your last will and testament.

Further, witnesses should not include anyone from within the medical community (physicians, nurses, hospital administrators) who may have an obvious conflict because the living will helps protect them from liability.

The attorney for personal care is not allowed to be a witness. In addition, neither the spouse of the person making the living will nor the spouse of the attorney for personal care can act as witnesses. This protects an individual from outside pressure to both draft a living will in the first place, and to choose a specific individual to make healthcare decisions for him or her. If the living will is witnessed by persons who are not legally bound to either its author or attorney for personal care, this pressure is less likely to occur.

Storing your living will

Properly signed and witnessed, copies of your living will should be left with the patient's family, physician and in the medical records in the hospital to ensure availability at the appropriate time. Notify your family and physician (particularly the appointed decision-makers) that you have made a living will. Place the original living will in a safe place, but not in a safety deposit box. Otherwise, your appointed decision-maker may not have access to it.

Revoking or revising a living will

There are a number of ways to revoke a living will. The patient may simply tear it up or mark it "revoked" or "cancelled." The patient may simply request medical care inconsistent with the living will, thereby nullifying the living will. A court may also invalidate a living will made years earlier when the patient's circumstances may have 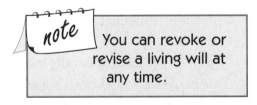 been different. This underlines the need for the patient to periodically update any living will as an expression of current intent.

note

You can revoke or revise a living will at any time.

Review your living will when:

- your medical condition changes

- you are admitted to a hospital

- you marry or divorce

- you move to another province

HOT **spot** Be certain to notify all parties who were notified of the earlier living will when you revoke a living will or replace it with a new one.

Keep up-to-date about new medical treatments for conditions and illnesses you may have. Alter your living will to reflect current changes if there are optional treatments for your condition.

When does your living will and power of attorney for personal care take effect?

When do you want your attorney for personal care to take over? When do you want him or her to "pull the plug"? You want to ensure that no one abuses his or her powers or intervenes without necessity. There have been many court battles between children who cannot concur when their mother or father have become incompetent, and summon medical experts to justify their respective positions.

Spouses generally trust the other to decide when to "pull the plug." If not married or without a significant other, you may leave the decision to a doctor. Some provinces, such as Ontario, have specific procedures and definitions to determine when you become incapable. In any case, choose the attorney for personal care whom you feel most comfortable with and whom you trust will follow your wishes at the appropriate time.

When you become incapacitated and cannot make your own medical decisions, a healthcare worker—usually a doctor—requests someone to either consent to or deny further treatment on your behalf. This is when your power of attorney for personal care takes effect. The individual appointed in your power of attorney for personal care, in most provinces, must abide by the instructions contained in your living will rather than make any of his or her decisions. In other provinces, the decision-maker can consider the instructions contained in your living will, but has the authority to override them.

If your living will does not have instructions that cover the specific situation, the decision-maker should abide by the wishes conveyed to him or her before you became incapacitated. If you did not stipulate your wishes to your decision-maker, he or she must make a decision based on what he or she thinks you would want. However, if the decision-maker has no idea what your wishes would be, he or she must make an informed decision based upon the nature of the proposed treatment. Your decision-maker should consider whether the treatment will improve your quality of life—whether the treatment's benefits outweigh its risks.

How to complete your living will

Photocopy the living will, and it is ready to complete and use.

Step 1) **Personal Identification.** Sign and date the living will using your full legal name. You may type or print the name of anyone to whom you have given copies of your living will.

Step 2) **Acknowledgement Clause.** In the acknowledgement clause, the witnesses state that they signed their names in each other's presence and in the presence of the testator. The acknowledgement clause acts as an affidavit, so that when a will is signed and notarized, the witnesses usually do not have to appear in court.

Step 3)   **Witnesses**. You must sign in the presence of two disinterested witnesses. Each witness should in turn sign in your presence after you have signed, and in the presence of each other. Make certain that witnesses are disinterested. This means they should not be relatives, healthcare providers or others involved in your estate or legal financial affairs. The witnesses should also include their address and province.

Step 4)   **Affidavit of Execution** (optional). Your province may require that each witness complete a separate Affidavit of Execution.

Step 5)   **Make copies**. Make as many copies as you may need for family representatives and healthcare providers.

Step 6)   **Notify others.** It is important that your physician and family members know that you have prepared a living will so they can act on your wishes should the circumstances present themselves. You should send a copy of your living will to your primary physician, Also forward a copy to the hospital administrator if you know which hospital shall provide care for you.

Instructions for completing your living will

These instructions will guide you in filling in the blanks of the living will provided with this manual.

❶ Enter full legal name of testator.

❷ Enter name(s) and contact information for anyone receiving a copy of your living will.

❸ Enter the city where you reside.

❹ Enter the province where you reside.

❺ Enter the day, month, and year.

❻ Testator must sign in the presence of the witnesses.

❼ Enter the name of the testator.

❽ To be completed and signed by the witnesses.

Estate Planning

What is estate planning?

14

What is estate planning?

The purpose of estate planning is to maximize assets during your lifetime and then distribute them upon your death. It requires you to take stock of your assets, and provide for your dependents and loved ones when you are gone. It is the manner in which you decide who gets what from your estate. Such legal documents as a will and a living will, among others, constitute part of an estate plan.

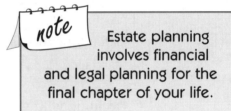

note Estate planning involves financial and legal planning for the final chapter of your life.

Distributing assets

You may distribute your assets through your will to your dependents. However, there are five other methods of transferring your estate:

- Through the *Laws of Intestate Succession* in your province should you die without a will

- By specifying heirs on life insurance policies, pension plans, RRSPs and RRIFs

- By giving them away during your lifetime

- Through joint ownership

- By spending more money on yourself while you are still alive

Moreover, estate planning involves much more than distributing your property through a will. It also includes:

- Satisfying your financial needs for the remainder of your life

- Designating authority to others to manage your medical and financial affairs should you become incapable of doing so

- Planning your funeral

- Providing for your family after you die

- Selecting a guardian for your children

- Defending the financial interests of your children from another marriage

- Deciding who will manage your business, if you have one

- Saving money on probate fees and income taxes

- Expediting the inheritance process

- Donating to charity

- Protecting your current and future assets

It is never too early to prepare an estate plan. Start planning as soon as you have accumulated assets or have started a family. Keep your estate plan effective and current by periodically revising it when financial or personal circumstances change.

Benefits of estate planning

An estate plan often prevents the government from interfering in your life. When you do not have an estate plan, government laws control your interests. These laws may not reflect your wishes. Your beneficiaries probably do not want a government official to make important decisions for them, and do not want to have to answer to him or her to validate their actions.

By properly planning your estate, you can:

- Leave your property to your desired beneficiaries

- Ensure you don't pay unnecessary taxes

- Leave enough money to pay your bills

- Decrease probate fees

- Contribute to charity

- Decrease Executor/Executrix/Trustee fees

- Employ income splitting methods

- Shield your assets from creditors

- Guarantee that your business continues without you

- Protect your assets from creditors or financial disaster

Types of property

Four categories of property exist that determine how your property will be handled upon death. Understand the legal implications of each, and you can make well-informed decisions that will benefit your estate.

1) **Solely owned property.** All the assets that you hold in your name only constitute solely owned property. For example, you may have bought a car in your name or you may have inherited a stock in your name. You should bequeath these types of assets in your will.

2) **Joint assets with right of survivorship.** Joint ownership with right of survivorship (also referred to as joint tenancy when owning a house) signifies that more than one person owns the assets, and they own them at the same time. Consequently, when one owner passes away, the living owner still possesses the assets, despite what the deceased's will states. Term deposits, guaranteed investment certificates, and Canada Savings Bonds may be held jointly. An elderly parent may name a child as a joint owner of a bank account or put his or her name on the title of the home. When the child has joint ownership with right of survivorship of the house, and the parent dies, the child automatically inherits the home.

note Many couples have joint ownership of their house and bank accounts.

3) **Designated beneficiary assets.** RRSPs, RRIFs, LIRAs, employer pensions, and life insurance benefits that are automatically transferred to a previously named individual are considered designated beneficiary assets. Their distribution is not conditional upon what you state in your will. The law permits you to assign or designate a beneficiary when you purchase the asset. You usually accomplish this by completing a section of a form, and signing it.

4) **A tenant-in-common** denotes that each of the purchasers owns a portion of the title to the property. When your co-owner passes away, you only retain your portion of the property—the other portion is left to his or her beneficiaries, and you then have new co-owners of the asset.

Protecting your assets

Protecting your assets

15

Joint ownership is particularly common amongst spouses, whether for titling the family home, bank accounts, shares in family-owned businesses, investments or works of art, collectibles, boats and autos. Co-ownership is also common between other family members. For example, a widowed mother may jointly title her assets with a daughter to avoid probate upon the mother's death. But we also see co-ownership arrangements between very sophisticated corporations.

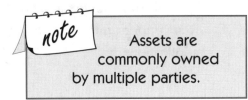

note

Assets are commonly owned by multiple parties.

Co-ownership

Co-owning property is an important asset protection strategy. However, incorrectly co-owning property will present greater dangers than owning the property outright or through an entity. The two most important questions when considering co-ownership are:

1) will co-ownership expand your liability (can you more readily lose your share of the co-owned assets to creditors?

2) will co-ownership give you the needed protection?

Converting individually owned property outright into assets co-owned with others, most likely your spouse, may be the simplest way to shelter these assets since it requires little effort or cost. So co-ownership may be one of the first strategies you consider for asset protection. But it has its limitations, and stronger asset protection measures are usually needed.

Co-ownership can make sense for reasons other than asset protection. It can help you avoid probate, since jointly owned property automatically passes to the surviving joint owner. Many families protected their assets from creditors only because their home, stocks, bonds or other important assets were co-owned. Asset protection was oftentimes the unintended but welcomed benefit. More knowledgeable individuals realize that co-ownership can also be an effective wealth insulator. Probate avoidance becomes their secondary goal; asset protection, their first!

To fully understand co-ownership strategies for asset protection, you must first understand the co-ownerships; their advantages, disadvantages, and applications.

Common dangers with tenancy-in-common

When two or more parties own property together as tenants-in-common, each tenant (co-owner) owns a divided interest in that property. That ownership interest is a divisible or dividable interest, and each co-tenant can sell, mortgage, bequeath or dispose of his share of the property without interference or the consent of co-owners.

Since the tenant-in-common's interest in the property is separate and apart from the interests of co-owners, his creditors can reach that divisible interest in the property. The interests of co-owners remain safe from everyone but their own creditors. Tenancy-in-common features absolutely no creditor protection.

Property owned as tenancy-in-common has other hazards. For example, when you own property as a tenant-in-common, your co-owner's creditors can petition the court for permission to sell the entire property through a forced liquidation of your co-owner's interest. You would no longer own a share of the property and instead receive proceeds from the sale that represent your interest. You may always negotiate the purchase of your co-owner's interest from his creditor, but that is not always possible, practical or desirable. Moreover, if the creditor (or any buyer of the debtor's interest in the property) did not want to sell his newly gained interest in the property, you may then end up with a stranger as your new co-owner.

Tenancy-in-common is not limited to two individuals. There can be many co-owners with each owning a different share of the property, although it is unwieldy to use tenancy-in-common with more than three or four co-owners. For multiple owners, use a corporation, limited partnership, trust, or some other entity to own the propert. Then there is less chance that title to the property will become clouded by the death or legal problems of one co-owner.

Your options as co-owner under a tenancy-in-common encountering financial problems are varied. One option is to transfer your interest to the other co-owner at a discount if necessary, before the property is claimed by your creditor. Once the creditor threat passes, the property can be reconveyed to the original co-owner.

Since property under tenancy-in-common is vulnerable to a forced liquidation to satisfy one co-owner's debts, it is important for co-owners under this tenancy to form their relationship confident that their respective finances are stable. This confidence can be misplaced. Parties with financial or legal problems should avoid a tenancy-in-common. Even with a good financial record, later problems may jeopardize co-owned property. And co-owners must always warn each other against foreseeable problems so they collectively and quickly can safeguard the property and their respective interests before they are endangered by a creditor.

A tenancy-in-common has no survivorship rights. Each co-owner's interest upon death will not pass to the surviving co-owner, but instead go to his heirs. However, this can cause still other complications since heirs seldom share the surviving co-owner's objectives with the property. A buy-out agreement between co-owners is one solution to this problem, particularly when the buy-out is funded by insurance, an arrangement more common with multi-stockholder businesses.

Joint tenancy: traps and opportunities

 **Definition:**

A *joint tenancy* is created when real or personal property is equally owned by two or more parties with the express provision that title is jointly held.

Most provinces require the joint tenancy to be created by written agreement. Verbal agreement is insufficient. This joint tenancy acknowledgment may be stated in the deed, bill of sale, or other title documents such as a stock certificate. (Example: Mary Doe and/or Ann Smith, jointly, or as joint tenants.) The "or" indicates survivorship rights, which does not apply to a tenancy-in-common. When one joint tenant dies, the surviving tenant or tenants automatically assumes ownership of the deceased tenant's interest, even if the decedent bequeathed his interest in the property to someone else. Jointly owned property avoids probate (but not estate taxes), and this is its chief advantage and reason for its popularity.

Joint tenancy grants each owner an equal and undivided interest in the property. But this joint tenancy can be terminated if either joint tenant conveys his interest. The joint tenancy then automatically ends and the remaining joint tenants become tenants-in-common with the new owner.

How effectively does joint tenancy protect assets? A joint tenancy usually provides little protection over a tenancy-in-common. Creditors of one joint tenant can ordinarily reach his undivided interest in the property by petitioning the court to partition the property and order its sale with the proceeds divided. Creditor protection with a joint tenancy can vary considerably among provinces.

Carefully check the laws in your province before you rely upon joint-tenancy to protect your assets.

Most provinces allow the debtor-joint tenant's interest to be reached by his creditors during his lifetime. Since each joint tenant, during this period, can freely transfer his interest, his creditors are allowed to reach that same interest to satisfy that joint tenant's debts. The creditor's forced-sale position places the creditor and his buyer in the same position as someone who buys the asset directly from the joint tenant: The joint tenancy is destroyed and the creditor or his nominee buyer becomes a tenant-in-common with other co-owners.

Creditors generally cannot proceed against jointly owned property once the debtor-joint tenant dies because his interest automatically passes to the other co-owners, but there are three important exceptions:

1) A joint tenancy expressly established to defraud creditors can be set aside; however, a joint tenancy does not evidence fraud.

2) Unlike other debts, federal and province taxes owed by a deceased joint tenant attach to the joint interest and pass with the property of the deceased to the surviving tenant.

3) Most assets, except for insurance, can be jointly owned. You can also avoid probate when all assets are jointly held. However, joint tenancy is not necessary to achieve asset protection and probate avoidance. For probate avoidance alone, you can title property in a living trust.

A creditor's rights against jointly held property ends with the death of the debtor. And an attachment during the debtor's lifetime must be liquidated through partition and sale of the property while the debtor remains alive because the debtor's joint interest automatically passes upon death to the surviving joint tenant, and the survivorship transfer would then extinguish the attachment and creditor's rights against that interest. Should the non-debtor joint tenant die first, the creditor would gain the entire property. Survivorship works both ways. Creditors with a judgment sometimes sit on their rights while awaiting the death of the other owner in a winner-take-all, particularly in provinces where joint tenancy effectively protects against creditors.

Avoid joint bank accounts

How safe are joint bank accounts? This is an important question considering their popularity between spouses, family members and even unrelated parties who live or conduct business together using joint accounts.

A creditor of one joint tenant can usually reach the entire bank account because the creditor's rights to the funds match those of the debtor-joint tenant. Since the debtor-joint tenant can withdraw the entire account, so can his creditor. A joint bank account then becomes dangerous since it is fully jeopardized for the debts of one party.

> **note** Whether creditors of one joint tenant to the bank account can seize all or part of such an account to satisfy the debt rests chiefly upon provincial law.

There are many other ways to lose jointly titled funds. You may, for example, share a joint bank account with your married son. Upon your death, the account avoids probate and automatically passes to your son. But should your son divorce, the wife may freeze the account until the divorce is finalized and the account may be awarded your daughter-in-law. A lawsuit will similarly jeopardize the account.

The risks associated with jointly held properties are not limited to bank accounts. What we say about bank accounts generally applies to such other jointly held property as stocks and bonds, collectibles, autos and boats.

There is also increased liability with jointly owned property. An auto is an example where both spouses become liable if the auto is involved in an accident.

HOT spot Avoid expanded liability. Do not jointly own vehicles and other assets that can create liability.

Co-ownerships avoid probate

Joint tenancy conveniently allows a husband and wife to avoid probate. However, there are safer ways to avoid probate. A living trust is one example because a living trust keeps assets safe from creditors of the other higher-risk spouse.

There can also be adverse tax consequences when you transfer property through rights of survivorship. Taxes may be eliminated or reduced through more creative trusts. A joint tenancy may also conflict with how you wish to bequeath your assets. An example is when you have children from a prior marriage to whom you want to leave assets. When you own property jointly with your second spouse, that property will automatically pass to that spouse upon your death, and eventually to his or her family. You may alternatively want to leave property to your new spouse under a life estate. Upon his or her death the assets then pass to your children. Joint ownership defeats such estate planning.

Whether joint tenancy is advantageous or disadvantageous can only be determined through a professional evaluation of your financial situation, your provincial laws, and your wealth-transfer objectives. The point is that you cannot simply assume co-ownerships are always advantageous, whether for estate planning or asset protection. Often it is disadvantageous while other strategies would more effectively produce the right results.

More reasons to avoid joint ownership

Aside from the reality that it offers questionable asset protection, there are other disadvantages of joint ownership:

- Co-owners can seldom transfer their interests without the consent from the other co-owner. This may prevent the timely transfer of property, whether for asset protection, estate planning or other purposes.

- The death of one co-owner can impede the other owner's use of the asset. Jointly owned bank accounts, for instance, are then usually frozen.

- Joint ownership can spread liability — as when a jointly owned auto or boat is involved in an accident.

Planning pointers

When you plan your estate, consider the advantages and disadvantages of different ownership types. Remember the following:

1) Co-ownership of assets may protect assets or expand liability and the potential loss of property—depending upon the asset, type of co-ownership, and provincial law.

2) Tenancy-in-common offers no asset protection and when one co-owner has creditors, it can disrupt the tenancy and force the sale of the co-owned asset.

3) Jointly owned property automatically bequeaths the interest of a deceased co-owner to the other co-owners, and this can avoid probate but not estate taxes.

4) Jointly owned property is generally not protected from creditors of a co-owner.

5) Joint bank accounts and joint ownership of other assets are particularly dangerous as a creditor of either joint owner can possibly assert claim to the entire asset, notwithstanding the relative contribution of either co-tenant.

Probate and probate-free assets

Probate-free assets do not involve the terms contained in your will. Probate-free assets are automatically transferred to a designated individual after your death, and avoid probate. Joint assets with right of survivorship and designated beneficiary assets are probate-free assets.

> *note*
> Probate and probate-free assets comprise the two possible types of assets that you may leave behind.

Assets in your name only and assets held as a tenant in common are probate assets. Account for these assets in your will as bequests. When you die without a will, your probate assets will be distributed according to your provincial intestate law.

When couples own only probate-free assets, why is estate planning, and specifically wills still necessary? You must consider every conceivable situation to protect your assets. Even if you both own only probate-free assets, without a will you have not covered what will happen to your estate if you both should die simultaneously. If you die simultaneously and have children, are they old enough to inherit money? Who will care for them? If you don't have children, who will inherit your property? What happens if you become incapable of making medical decisions? Your estate planning documents, i.e., a will and a living will, answer these questions, and legally protect you in the case of unforeseen circumstances.

Single people with no children must also consider estate planning techniques. To whom would you like to leave your assets? How do you want to be remembered? Who will make your medical decisions for you? These questions must be considered at some stage in your life.

Giving your assets away

People differ in their estate planning philosophies. Some people concern themselves with leaving money to their dependents, while others want to spend or give away all their money while they are still alive. The approach you take usually depends on how large your estate is, how old you are, and your health.

There may be several benefits to giving your assets away during your lifetime:

- Experience the gratitude of those charities and individuals you give to

- Decrease probate fees

- Decrease Executor/Executrix/Trustee fees

- Decrease future income taxes by giving a cash gift to an adult child

- Maximize tax savings by donating to charities

- Ensure the privacy of your gift giving

- Eliminate possible family feuds over your will

However, realize that there are also drawbacks to giving away portions of your estate while you are still alive:

- You would lose control over the asset or property. This may be a significant loss if it is a home or business.

- You might increase your income tax. If your gift's value increased since you obtained it, and you give it away at fair market value, Revenue Canada may deem the difference added taxable income.

- You may be taxed on any income earned on the asset that you give away due to Revenue Canada's attribution laws.

- You may not have enough money left to live on.

You may not give away your family home or your spouse's property without his or her agreement. You may give away gifts to children, nieces, nephews, grandchildren, friends or a charity. You may want to give money towards your child's or grandchild's first home, education, or school loan or help him or her start a new business.

How to give a gift

Certain provisions apply in order to make a valid gift. The gift must be valid for the new owner to have the legal right to sell it, mortgage it, or spend it.

To give a valid gift:

- You must own the property. You cannot gift your spouse's or children's property or property in which you share ownership (unless you receive his or her consent).

- You must intend to give away your control of property.

- You must hand over the gift and/or transfer title of property, if applicable. You must execute and deliver the title documents transferring ownership of a car, home or investment. You must make arrangements for delivery or pick up of furniture.

- You must make sure the recipient will accept the gift.

In addition to the legal requirements for a valid gift, you must give the gift on your own accord. This means:

- You must be mentally capable. In order to have the required intention for gift-giving, you must be capable of comprehending the legal and practical implications of giving the gift.

- You must not be forced or threatened to make the gift (under duress).

- You must not be pressured by the recipient to make the gift (under undue influence).

If you give a gift when you are mentally incompetent, under duress, or under undue influence, you may apply to the court to revoke your gift and get it back (once you have regained mental competence).

Gift taxes

When you contemplate leaving your assets to your heirs, consider the issue of taxes. If you can afford to do it, there are two possible tax benefits to giving away assets in the form of gifts during your lifetime:

- **You may save your estate capital gains taxes.** Your estate pays capital gains taxes only on what you own at the time of your death. When you give away assets as gifts, the assets are considered sold and deducted from the value of your estate. The less you own at the time of death, the less estate taxes you owe.

- **You may save income tax.** When you part with property that presently produces income, future income earned from that property belongs to the new owner who is now responsible for paying taxes on the increased income. Your income decreases, and you pay less income taxes.

These are possible not definite ways of saving taxes. The tax laws take into account to whom you are giving your property. For example, when you give property to your spouse, and he or she sells it for a profit before your death, you may be responsible for the capital gains tax. This is known as attribution. Also, when you give income-earning property or a trust to your spouse, you are taxed on any interest, dividends, or capital gains from that property or trust. When you give income-earning property to a minor (under 18), you will be responsible for taxes on the interest or dividends. However, when you transfer income-earning property to an adult child or grandchild, you cannot be taxed on it.

If you contemplate transferring property, consider how much the value of the property will increase. If you think it will increase significantly before you die, it may be worthwhile to pay capital gains taxes now, and hold on to it. If you have other holdings with capital losses, give them away first to offset the capital gains earned on the profitable property, and, thus, pay no taxes.

If you are still concerned with your estate's capital gains taxes, be aware that your estate will not have to pay capital gains taxes on cash, treasury bills or any other investments that you give away that are essentially cash. Why? Because these assets do not increase in value. However, when you give away property such as investments, artwork, and real estate that does increase in value your estate is subject to capital gains taxes due to Revenue Canada's attribution laws. After death, Canada's attribution laws no longer apply.

Trusts and life insurance

16

16

Trusts and life insurance

A testamentary trust is similar to a last will and testament because it becomes effective after your death. Your estate is a form of testamentary trust as assets and property are retained before the beneficiaries receive them. The trustee of a testamentary trust and your Executor/Executrix are often the same person. However, a testamentary trust can last for many years after your death.

Common trusts

The most familiar kinds of testamentary trusts are the spousal trust and family trusts. Family trusts consist of:

- Trusts for minor children who are not entitled to hold assets directly

- Trusts for spendthrifts

- Trusts for family members who have special requirements

If you wish to form a testamentary trust, leave directions in your last will and testament. Appoint a trustee, designate the beneficiaries, assign which assets are to be included in the trust, and indicate how they are to be managed and distributed. You may modify the conditions of a trust by revising your will, either by creating a new will or adding a codicil to your present will.

Spousal Trusts

A spousal trust retains property and assets for the sole use by a surviving spouse. You may form a spousal trust with any or all of your inheritance. Originally, spousal trusts were established for widows who were incapable of managing their inherited assets.

Presently, their special uses include:

- **Income splitting.** When your spouse has an income of his or her own, the return on a bequeathed investment is added to his or her income and taxed. When you leave the money in a spousal trust, two income tax returns are filed—one for his or her income and one for the trust. This may result in less income tax to pay.

- **Remarriage.** If your surviving spouse remarries, a spousal trust provides for him or her and maintains the trust assets for your children.

- **Children from a previous marriage.** A spousal trust ensures that your children from a previous marriage will obtain assets, and your spouse will be taken care of. How? A spousal trust can establish an income for life for your spouse with the provision that upon his or her death, the remaining assets go to your children. This eliminates your children's need for relying on the good-will or last will of a step-parent

- **Probate fees.** You can eliminate your beneficiaries' having to pay probate fees twice by forming a spousal trust. For example, if you bequeath $50,000 to your spouse, probate fees will be assessed on that amount. When he or she dies, probate fees will be charged again. When you create a spousal trust with the funds to be held until his or her death, your children inherit the sum according to the trust agreement and avoid another probate fee

Family Trusts

Trusts may be created for other family members besides a spouse—young children or handicapped children. Testamentary trusts can also lower taxes. Establish the rules and conditions for the trust with carefully worded instructions in your will.

Since children are not legally permitted to own assets or property until the age of majority, it becomes necessary to establish a trust for them and name a trustee to handle their money. If you leave them an inheritance and it is not in a trust, the government will hold the money in trust for them and act as trustee until the children reach the age of majority. Then, the government would administer the trust to them in one lump sum. You may not want your 18-year-old to receive an inheritance in this manner.

In your will, you can establish a testamentary trust and dictate how and when the money will be distributed. You might specify that:

- Income accumulated by the trust is given to the child annually but the principal is to be withheld until a certain age conditioned upon specific circumstances

- The trustee distributes the trust's assets based upon his or her discretion

- The income from the trust and the principal can be distributed at any time only if it is for educational purposes.

Establishing a testamentary trust for grandchildren may yield income splitting for the family. When you leave the trust to your children (for your grandchildren's benefit), and the income earned from the trust is added to your children's income, a higher tax may be paid than if you left it to your grandchildren directly. In the latter case, you may appoint your children as the trustee if you believe they will act in the best interests of your grandchildren.

Consider creating a testamentary trust for children over 18 to guard these funds from your children's creditors and/or from a divorce settlement. You might also want to discuss asset protection strategies with your children to avoid exposing these assets to creditors or lawsuits.

A spendthrift trust, also known as a protective trust, is another type of family testamentary trust specially designed for individuals who may not be able to manage their inheritance if they acquired it directly. Suppose you have a son who has declared bankruptcy. You feel that if you bequeathed him money directly, he would waste it. By establishing a testamentary trust and appointing a trustee to administer it, he would receive the income from the assets, but the trustee would have control over the assets themselves.

If you have a handicapped child, either physically or mentally, who is dependent upon you and unable to manage his or her own financial matters, establish a testamentary trust to provide funds for him or her after your death. You may also want to provide a testamentary trust for an elderly parent. Suppose your child worked at home because of an illness, which could worsen at any time. You may want to establish a testamentary trust for him or her in the event he or she can no longer work. In this case, be sure to designate beneficiaries for this type of testamentary trust.

If the disabled child cannot work at all and receives social assistance, an inheritance may affect his or her qualifications for government assistance. Discuss this situation with a lawyer to determine a trust that can be formed where your handicapped child will not lose his or her benefits.

Life insurance

When you take out a life insurance policy, you (as owner) legally agree to pay premiums to the insurance company in exchange for the insurance company's pledge to pay a specific amount of money (the policy's face amount) to a designated person (the *beneficiary*) upon your death. The face amount is not taxed when it is paid.

Your beneficiary may own the policy on your life and pay the premiums. However, not everyone can take out a life insurance policy for another individual. The owner of the policy must have a personal or business relationship with the person whose life he or she is insuring. This *insurable interest* ensures the insurance company that the policy owner wants the insured to remain alive.

Is life insurance necessary?

To determine whether you need life insurance, get acquainted with the common uses of life insurance:

- To substitute the income you would have earned if alive for the dependents you leave behind. This ensures that they will be able to maintain their present lifestyle.

- To pay off a mortgage, a loan (personal or business), or provide for the university education for your children. Without life insurance, your family may have to dip into the estate's principal to meet these expenses.

- To settle your estate and pay funeral costs, lawyer's fees, taxes, and probate fees. Your estate incurs these fees upon your death, and they are usually deducted from the estate.

- To provide extra money to a family member, friend, or charity. You may want to give more money than you presently have.

Life insurance is not necessary when you:

- Don't have dependents

- Don't owe money

- Don't have expenses

- Don't need the extra money to pay for death-related expenses

- Don't want to leave more money to family, friends, or charities.

> **HOT spot** You do not need life insurance if you have enough money in your estate to adequately provide for your dependents and pay off large debts, expenses, and taxes.

How much life insurance should you buy?

If you have decided that you need life insurance, determine how much you can presently manage to pay and then the actual amount you want. Consider the reason for taking out the policy:

- You want to replace your income so that your dependents can live like they are accustomed to. How much life insurance will that require? Subtract your family's expenses from the other income they will receive without your present salary. Determine if there will be a shortfall between your family's expenses and income, and, if so, take out enough life insurance to make up the difference.

- You want to pay a debt or expense. Take out a policy equal to the cost of a mortgage or university education for your children, if you do not have enough money in your estate to cover such debts or expenses.

- You want to leave money to specific individuals. Take out a policy in the amount of the desired bequest.

Naming your beneficiary

After calculating how much life insurance to buy, you must then choose a beneficiary who will receive the proceeds of the life insurance policy upon your death. Again, consider why you are taking out the insurance before you name your beneficiary. You can appoint a beneficiary in three ways:

Select a beneficiary prudently, and keep in mind your estate planning objectives.

- Name an individual (or two or more)

- Name your estate

- Form an insurance trust and instruct the insurance company to pay the proceeds directly to a trustee who will maintain them for your beneficiary

Let's look at each option individually.

Naming an individual. When you select an individual as your beneficiary, he or she will receive the proceeds from the insurance company upon your death. That money is not considered part of your estate, and may not be used to pay off the estate's debts. It is also not subject to probate fees. Your beneficiary requests the money from the insurance company and need not wait for your Executor/Executrix/Trustee to distribute the money from the estate. When you select a minor as your beneficiary, the proceeds are paid to the court, and a government official holds the money until the child reaches the age of majority.

Naming your estate as your beneficiary. When you designate your estate as your beneficiary, the insurance proceeds go to your Executor/Executrix/ Trustee and become part of your estate. Be sure to further instruct in your will whom you want this money left to. If you don't have a will, the proceeds will be allocated to your family according to your provincial intestate law. Also, unlike naming an individual as a beneficiary, when you name your estate as your beneficiary, the insurance money may be applied towards your debts. After all, your Executor/Executrix/Trustee must pay your debts before distributing your bequests. Therefore, your proceeds may go to your creditors rather than your loved ones. In addition, the proceeds are probated. This means that the fees paid to the court based on the value of the estate (probate fees) include the proceeds from your life insurance policy. Consequently, the probate fees would be higher. Probate fees are deducted from the estate.

Forming an insurance trust. When you form an insurance trust, you essentially designate a trustee to hold the proceeds for your beneficiaries. Create an insurance trust for young children when you want to leave money for your children, but you don't want the government to handle the money until they reach the age of majority. Also, provide directions to your trustee regarding what he or she should do with the money until your children can inherit it. For example, you might tell your trustee to invest the money in the meantime, and use the money earned on the investment towards your children's expenses. An insurance trust may also act in the same manner as a will—you can divide your proceeds. Your Executor/Executrix/Trustee may act as trustee for the insurance trust. Depending on how they are worded, some insurance trusts will not be assessed as part of your estate, and, therefore, not liable for either probate fees or creditors' claims. Consult with a lawyer to prepare a separate trust agreement or include a trust in your will.

HOT spot Remember, inform the insurance company to pay the proceeds to your trustee upon your death.

Have you achieved a sense of accomplishment by completing your estate plan and documenting your wishes in your living will and last will and testament? After all, you have just designed a plan that covers your needs for the final chapter of your life, and provided for your loved ones after you are gone.

The forms
in this Kit

Last Will and Testament and Instructions 205

Affidavit of Execution for Witness 209

Statement of Wishes 210

Personal Information 211

Funeral Requests 212

Notification List 213

Document Locator 214

Insurance/Pension Data 215

Schedule of Assets 216

Living Will and Instructions...217

Power of Attorney for Personal Care 219

About These Forms:
While the legal forms and documents in this product generally conform to the requirements of courts nationwide, certain courts may have additional requirements. Before completing and filing the forms in this product, check with the clerk of the court concerning these requirements.

LAST WILL AND TESTAMENT

How to complete...

LAST WILL AND TESTAMENT
OF
❶
_____

This is the Last Will of me, **❷** ,
resident of **❸**
❹ (city), **❺** (province),
made this **❻** ay of **❼** , 2 **❽** revoke all my prior wills and codicils.

1.   I appoint **❾**
of **❿** (city), **⓫** (province),
to be my Executor/Executrix and Trustee. If **⓬** is unwilling or unable to
act or to continue to act as my Executor/Executrix and Trustee, I appoint **⓭**
⓯ , of **⓮**
(city), **⓰** (province),
to be my Executor/Executrix and Trustee.

2.   I give my Executor/Executrix and Trustee all my property of every kind and
wherever located to administer as I direct in this Will. My Executor/Executrix and
Trustee shall be authorized to carry out all terms of this Will and pay my just debts,
obligations and funeral expenses.

3.   Bequests: After payment of my debts, I direct that my property be bequeathed as
follows:
⓱

Page ___ of ___ **⓲**   Testator's Initials **⓳**   Witness' Initials **⓴**   Witness' Initials **㉑**

❶ Type or print your name on the center top line so the will is identified as yours
❷ Restate your name
❸ Enter the street address where you reside
❹ Enter the city where you reside
❺ Enter the province where you reside, if applicable. This is where your will may be probated
❻ Enter the number of the day
❼ Enter the month
❽ Enter the year
❾ Identify whom you wish to appoint as your Executor/Trustee or Executrix/Trustee
❿ Enter the city of your Executor/Trustee or Executrix/Trustee
⓫ Enter the province of your Executor/Trustee or Executrix/Trustee
⓬ Enter the name of your Executor/Trustee or Executrix/Trustee
⓭ Enter the name of alternate Executor/Trustee or Executrix/Trustee, should your first named Executor/Trustee or Executrix/Trustee be unable or unwilling to serve
⓮ Enter the street address of alternate Executor/Trustee or Executrix/Trustee
⓯ Enter the city of alternate Executor/Trustee or Executrix/Trustee
⓰ Enter the province of alternate Executor/Trustee or Executrix/Trustee
⓱ List your special bequests. Note that the sample will only contains two special bequests, but you may have many such bequests
⓲ Number each page: i.e. page one of two, page three of eight
⓳ Testator initials here
⓴ 1st witness initials here
㉑ 2nd witness initials here

Orig. 06/01

4.   Debts to be Paid From My Estate: Pay out of my estate the following: .

(22)

5.   Residue of Estate: I give the residue of my estate to **(23)**   ,
if **(24)**   survives me for 30 days; if **(25)**   does
not survive me for 30 days, to divide the residue of my estate into as many equal shares
as I have children who survive me, except if any child of mine dies before me and leaves
one or more of his or her children alive at my death, an equal share will also be created
for that deceased child.

IN WITNESS WHEREOF I have signed my name to this and the preceding **(26)** pages at
(27)   (city), **(28)**   (province), this **(29)** day of
(30)   , 2 **(31)**   .

_____
                                                                (32)
                                                        Testator's Signature

We were both present, at the request of
(33)   ,
when he/she signed this Will. We then
signed as witnesses in his/her presence
and in the presence of each other.

_____   _____
Signature of Witness   **(34)** Signature of Witness

_____   _____
Printed Name   Printed Name

_____   _____
Address (Street)   Address (Street)

_____   _____
City   City

_____   _____
Province   Province

(18)   **(35)**   **(36)**   **(37)**
Page ___ of ___ Testator's Initials   Witness' Initials Witness' Initials

(22) List outstanding debts you wish your estate to pay

(23) Enter the name of the person(s) to receive the rest of your estate after the specific bequests have been distributed and debts paid

(24) Enter appropriate pronoun

(25) Enter the name of the person(s) to receive the rest of your estate after the specific bequests have been distributed and debts paid

(26) Enter the number of preceding pages

(27) Enter the city in which you are signing this will

(28) Enter the province in which you are signing this will

(29) Enter the number of the day

(30) Enter the month

(31) Enter the year

(32) Sign your will exactly as your name first appears. Be sure you sign in the presence of your witnesses

(33) Enter the name of the testator

(34) Each witness should sign his or her full name and complete address. Make certain your witnesses are disinterested parties and sign in each other's presence after the testator signs and in the presence of the testator

(18) Number each page: i.e. page one of two, page three of eight

(35) Testator initials here

(36) 1st witness initials here

(37) 2nd witness initials here

Bear in mind: That your will may contain other types of provisions. You may, for example, desire to have property held in trust for a beneficiary. These and other possible provisions should be carefully considered before drafting your will.

Don't forget: Schedule a review of your will each year so it remains up-to-date.

Note: File a *Wills Notice* with the appropriate government agency if applicable in your province.

LAST WILL AND TESTAMENT
OF

This is the Last Will of me,   ,
resident of   ,
                              (city),   (province),
made this   day of   , 2   . I revoke all my prior wills and codicils.

1.   I appoint   ,
of   (city),   (province),
to be my Executor/Executrix and Trustee. If   is unwilling or unable to
act or to continue to act as my Executor/Executrix and Trustee, I appoint
                    , of   ,
                              (city),   (province),
to be my Executor/Executrix and Trustee.

2. I give my Executor/Executrix and Trustee all my property of every kind and wherever located to
administer as I direct in this Will. My Executor/Executrix and Trustee shall be authorized to carry out
all terms of this Will and pay my just debts, obligations and funeral expenses.

3.   Bequests: After payment of my debts, I direct that my property be bequeathed as follows:

Page ___ of ___   Testator's Initials   Witness' Initials   Witness' Initials

4.   Debts to be Paid From My Estate: Pay out of my estate the following:

5.   Residue of Estate: I give the residue of my estate to   ,
if   survives me for 30 days; if   does
not survive me for 30 days, to divide the residue of my estate into as many equal shares
as I have children who survive me, except if any child of mine dies before me and leaves
one or more of his or her children alive at my death, an equal share will also be created
for that deceased child.

IN WITNESS WHEREOF I have signed my name to this and the preceding   pages at
                              (city),   (province), this   day of
            , 2   .

_____
                                        Testator's Signature

We were both present, at the request of

                                                ,

when he/she signed this Will. We then
signed as witnesses in his/her presence
and in the presence of each other.

_____   _____
Signature of Witness   Signature of Witness

_____   _____
Printed Name   Printed Name

_____   _____
Address (Street)   Address (Street)

_____   _____
City   City

_____   _____
Province   Province

Page ___ of ___   _____   _____   _____
                     Testator's Initials   Witness' Initials   Witness' Initials

AFFIDAVIT OF EXECUTION FOR WITNESS

I,   of   , in the
Province of   ,

MAKE OATH AND SAY:

1.   I was personally present and did see   , named in the attached
document, who is personally known to me to be the person named therein, duly sign and execute
the document for the purposes named therein.

2.   That the document was signed at   , in the Province of
, and that I am the subscribing witness thereto.

3.   That I know the person and he/she is in my belief of the full age of majority.

SWORN BEFORE ME at the
City of   ,   )
in the Province of   ,   )
this   day of   ,   )
A.D.   ) _____
)

_____
(Name of Commissioner or Notary)
My Commission Expires _____

STATEMENT OF WISHES
OF

     I,   , do hereby set forth certain wishes and requests to my personal representatives, heirs, family, friends and others who may carry out these wishes. I understand that these wishes are advisory only and not mandatory.

     My wishes are:

Dated:

_____
Signature

PERSONAL INFORMATION

Full Legal Name:

Address:

Social Insurance No.:   Spouse:

Armed Forces Service No.:

Date and Location of Discharge:

Birth Date: Marriage Date:

Father's Full Name:

Mother's Full Maiden Name:

    Widowed: ❑   Separated: ❑   Divorced: ❑   Date:

Location of Separation Agreement/Divorce Decree:

Remarried? Yes ❑   No ❑   Date:

Children:

Name   Address   Birth Date

WILL

Location of Original Last Will:

Dated:

Codicil Completed? Yes ❑   No ❑ If Yes, Location:

Dated:

Location of Any Documents Mentioned in Will:

Dated:

FUNERAL REQUESTS
OF

Funeral Home:

Director: Telephone:

Address:

Service Type: Religious: ❏   Military: ❏   Fraternal: ❏

Person Officiating: Telephone:

Music Selections:

Reading Selections:

Flowers:

Memorials:

Pallbearers:

Disposition: Burial: ❏   Cremation: ❏

Other Instructions:

BURIAL

Cemetery:

Location:

Section: Plot No.:   Block:

Location of Deed:

Special Instructions:

FUNERAL EXPENSES COVERAGE

Life Insurance:

Social Insurance: Veteran's Administration:

Union Benefit: Fraternal Organization(s):

Pension Benefit:

Burial Insurance:

NOTIFICATION LIST

Accountant:

Attorney:

Banker:

Clergyman:

Executor/Executrix/Trustee:

Alternate Executor/Executrix/Trustee:

Funeral Director:

Guardian:

Alternate Guardian:

Insurance Agent:

Insurance Underwriter:

DOCUMENT LOCATOR
OF

Insurance Documents:

Birth Certificate:

Statement of Wishes:

Marriage License or Certificate:

Social Insurance Cards:

Military Records:

Divorce Decree:

Mortgage Documents:

Bank Passbooks:

Passport(s):

Tax Returns:

Will(s) and Trust(s):

Pre-Nuptial Agreement:

Business Papers:

Death Certificates:

Cemetery Deeds:

Warranties:

Stock Certificates:

Other Investment Certificates:

Letters of Final Request:

Anatomical Gift Authorization:

Citizenship Papers:

Safe Deposit Keys:

Financial Records:

INSURANCE/PENSION DATA

LIFE INSURANCE POLICIES

Company:

Agent: Telephone:

Policy Number: Date:

Amount: Owner:

Location of Policy:

Beneficiary:

Company:

Agent: Telephone:

Policy Number: Date:

Amount: Owner:

Location of Policy:

Beneficiary:

Company:

Agent: Telephone:

Policy Number: Date:

Amount: Owner:

Location of Policy:

Beneficiary:

PENSIONS/ANNUITIES

Company:

Contract: Telephone:

Company:

Contract: Telephone:

SCHEDULE OF ASSETS

Name of Testator:
Date of Will:

No.	Description of item	Form of ownership	Replacement cost

LIVING WILL

How to complete...

Living Will Declaration

To my family, my physician, my lawyer, my clergyman. To any medical facility in whose care I happen to be. To any individual who may become responsible for my health, welfare or affairs.

Death is as much a reality as birth, growth, maturity and old age—it is the one certainty of life. If the time comes when I **❶** _____, can no longer take part in decisions of my own future, let this statement stand as an expression of my wishes, while I am still of sound mind.

If the situation should arise in which I am in a terminal state and there is no reasonable expectation of my recovery, I direct that I be allowed to die a natural death and that my life not be prolonged by extraordinary means. I do, however, ask that medication be mercifully administered to me to alleviate suffering even though this may shorten my remaining life.

This statement is made after careful consideration and is in accordance with my strong convictions and beliefs. I want the wishes and directions here expressed carried out to the extent permitted by law. Insofar as they are not legally enforceable, I hope that those to whom this will is addressed will regard themselves as morally bound by these provisions.

Copies of this request have been given to:

❷

IN WITNESS WHEREOF I have signed my name to this pages at **❸**
(city), **❹** (province),
this **❺** day of **❺** , 20 **❺**.

_____
❻
Testator's Signature

We were both present, at the request of

❼
when he/she signed this Living Will.
We then signed as witnesses in his/her presence and in the presence of each other.

_____
Signature of Witness

❽ _____
Signature of Witness

_____
Printed Name

_____
Printed Name

_____
Address (Street)

_____
Address (Street)

_____
City

_____
City

_____
Province

_____
Province

❶ Enter full legal name of testator

❷ Enter name(s) and contact information for anyone receiving a copy of your living will

❸ Enter the city where you reside

❹ Enter the province where you reside

❺ Enter the day, month, and year

❻ Testator must sign in the presence of the witnesses

❼ Enter the name of the testator

❽ To be completed and signed by the witnesses

Living Will Declaration

To my family, my physician, my lawyer, my clergyman. To any medical facility in whose care I happen to be. To any individual who may become responsible for my health, welfare or affairs.

Death is as much a reality as birth, growth, maturity and old age—it is the one certainty of life. If the time comes when I _____, can no longer take part in decisions of my own future, let this statement stand as an expression of my wishes, while I am still of sound mind.

If the situation should arise in which I am in a terminal state and there is no reasonable expectation of my recovery, I direct that I be allowed to die a natural death and that my life not be prolonged by extraordinary means. I do, however, ask that medication be mercifully administered to me to alleviate suffering even though this may shorten my remaining life.

This statement is made after careful consideration and is in accordance with my strong convictions and beliefs. I want the wishes and directions here expressed carried out to the extent permitted by law. Insofar as they are not legally enforceable, I hope that those to whom this will is addressed will regard themselves as morally bound by these provisions.

Copies of this request have been given to:

IN WITNESS WHEREOF I have signed my name to this pages at

(city),   (province),

this   day of   , 20   .

-_____

Testator's Signature

We were both present, at the request of

when he/she signed this Living Will.
We then signed as witnesses in his/her
presence and in the presence of each other.

_____   _____
Signature of Witness   Signature of Witness

_____   _____
Printed Name   Printed Name

_____   _____
Address (Street)   Address (Street)

_____   _____
City   City

_____   _____
Province   Province

Power of Attorney for Personal Care

How to complete...

Form (left page)

1. DESIGNATION OF PERSONAL CARE AGENT.
I,_____
(insert your name)
do hereby designate and appoint:
Name:_____
Address:_____
Telephone Number:_____
as my Agent to make personal care decisions for me as authorized in this document.

(Insert the name and address of the person you wish to designate as your Agent to make personal care decisions for you. Unless the person is also your spouse, legal guardian or the person most closely related to you by blood, **none** of the following may be designated as your Agent: (1) your treating provider of personal care, (2) an employee of your treating provider of personal care, (3) an operator of a community care or residential care facility, or (4) an employee of an operator of a community care or residential care facility.)

2. CREATION OF A POWER OF ATTORNEY FOR PERSONAL CARE.
By this document I intend to create a power of attorney by appointing the person designated above to make personal care decisions for me. This power of attorney shall not be affected by my subsequent incapacity.

3. GENERAL STATEMENT OF AUTHORITY GRANTED.
In the event that I am incapable of giving informed consent with respect to personal care decisions, I hereby grant to the Agent named above full power and authority to make personal care decisions for me before, or after my death, including: consent, refusal of consent, or withdrawal of consent to any care, treatment, service, or procedure to maintain, diagnose, or treat a physical or mental condition, subject only to the limitations and special provisions, if any, set forth in paragraph 4 or 6.

4. SPECIAL PROVISIONS AND LIMITATIONS.
(Your Agent is not permitted to consent to any of the following: commitment to or placement in a mental health treatment facility, convulsive treatment, psychosurgery, sterilization, or abortion. If there are any other types of treatment or placement that you do not want your agent's authority to give consent for or other restrictions you wish to place on your Agent's authority, you should list them in the space below. If you do not write any limitations, your Agent will have the broad powers to make personal care decisions on your behalf which are set forth in paragraph 3, except to the extent that there are limits provided by law.)

In exercising the authority under this power of attorney for personal care, the authority of my Agent is subject to the following special provisions and limitations:
_____
_____
_____
_____
_____

Orig. 9/01

Instructions (right column)

1. Insert your name
2. Insert the name of your personal care agent
3. Insert the address of personal care agent
4. Insert the telephone number of your personal care agent
5. List restrictions to your personal care agent's Authority
6. Only enter an expiration date if you want the Power of Attorney For Personal Care to expire on that exact date.
7. Check appropriate boxes indicating your refusal or consent to medical treatment
8. Enter additional wishes regarding treatment

Form (right page)

5. DURATION.
I understand that this power of attorney will exist indefinitely from the date I execute this document unless I establish a shorter time. If I am unable to make personal care decisions for myself when this power of attorney expires, the authority I have granted my Agent will continue to exist until the time when I become able to make personal care decisions for myself.
I wish to have this power of attorney end on the following date:_____
(Fill in expiration date if applicable)

6. STATEMENT OF DESIRES.
(With respect to decisions to withhold or withdraw life-sustaining treatment, your Agent must make personal care decisions that are consistent with your known desires. You can, but are not required to, indicate your desires below. If your desires are unknown, your Agent has the duty to act in your best interests; and, under some circumstances, a judicial proceeding may be necessary so that a court can determine the personal care decision that is in your best interests. If you wish to indicate your desires, you may INITIAL the statement or statements that reflect your desires and/or write your own statements in the space below.)

I direct my attending physician to withhold or withdraw life-sustaining treatment that serves only to prolong the process of my dying, if I should be in a terminal condition or in a state of permanent unconsciousness. I direct that treatment be limited to measures to keep me comfortable and to relieve pain, including any pain that might occur by withholding or withdrawing life-sustaining treatment.

In addition, if I am in the condition described above, I feel especially strong about the following forms of treatment:

I (   ) do (   ) do not want cardiac resuscitation.

I (   ) do (   ) do not want mechanical respiration.

I (   ) do (   ) do not want tube feeding or any other artificial or invasive form of nutrition (food) or hydration (water).

I (   ) do (   ) do not want blood or blood products.

I (   ) do (   ) do not want any form of surgery or invasive diagnostic tests.

I (   ) do (   ) do not want kidney dialysis.

I (   ) do (   ) do not want antibiotics.

I realize that if I do not specifically indicate my preference regarding any of the forms of treatment listed above, I may receive that form of treatment.
(If you wish to change your answer, you may do so by drawing an "X" through the answer you do not want, and circling the answer you prefer.)

Other or Additional Statements of Desires:_____
_____
_____
_____
_____

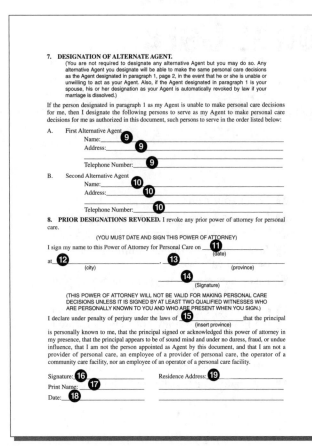

7. DESIGNATION OF ALTERNATE AGENT.
(You are not required to designate any alternative Agent but you may do so. Any alternative Agent you designate will be able to make the same personal care decisions as the Agent designated in paragraph 1, page 2, in the event that he or she is unable or unwilling to act as your Agent. Also, if the Agent designated in paragraph 1 is your spouse, his or her designation as your Agent is automatically revoked by law if your marriage is dissolved.)

If the person designated in paragraph 1 as my Agent is unable to make personal care decisions for me, then I designate the following persons to serve as my Agent to make personal care decisions for me as authorized in this document, such persons to serve in the order listed below:

A.   First Alternative Agent
      Name: ❾ _____
      Address: ❾ _____
      _____
      Telephone Number: ❾ _____

B.   Second Alternative Agent
      Name: ❿ _____
      Address: ❿ _____
      _____
      Telephone Number: ❿ _____

8. PRIOR DESIGNATIONS REVOKED. I revoke any prior power of attorney for personal care.

(YOU MUST DATE AND SIGN THIS POWER OF ATTORNEY)

I sign my name to this Power of Attorney for Personal Care on ⓫ _____
                                                              (date)

at ⓬ _____ , ⓭ _____
      (city)   (province)

⓮ _____
      (Signature)

(THIS POWER OF ATTORNEY WILL NOT BE VALID FOR MAKING PERSONAL CARE DECISIONS UNLESS IT IS SIGNED BY AT LEAST TWO QUALIFIED WITNESSES WHO ARE PERSONALLY KNOWN TO YOU AND WHO ARE PRESENT WHEN YOU SIGN.)

I declare under penalty of perjury under the laws of ⓯ _____ that the principal
                                                          (insert province)

is personally known to me, that the principal signed or acknowledged this power of attorney in my presence, that the principal appears to be of sound mind and under no duress, fraud, or undue influence, that I am not the person appointed as Agent by this document, and that I am not a provider of personal care, an employee of a provider of personal care, the operator of a community care facility, nor an employee of an operator of a personal care facility.

Signature: ⓰ _____   Residence Address: ⓳ _____
Print Name: ⓱ _____
Date: ⓲ _____   _____

---

❾ Enter name, address, and telephone number of first alternative agent

❿ Enter name, address, and telephone number of second alternative agent

⓫ Enter date when Power of Attorney for Personal Care is signed

⓬ Enter city where Power of Attorney for Personal Care is signed

⓭ Enter province where Power of Attorney for Personal Care is signed

⓮ Sign your name in the presence of at least two qualified witnesses

⓯ Insert province where Power of Attorney for Personal Care is signed

⓰ Signature of first witness

⓱ Print name of first witness

⓲ Enter date the first witness signed

⓳ Enter address of first witness

⓴ Signature of second witness

㉑ Print name of second witness

㉒ Enter date the second witness signed

㉓ Enter address of second witness

㉔ Enter province where Power of Attorney for Personal Care is signed

㉕ Enter signature of witness signing declaration

㉖ Print name of witness signing declaration

㉗ Enter date when declaration is signed

㉘ Enter address where declaration is signed

Signature: ⓴ _____   Residence Address: ㉓ _____
Print Name: ㉑ _____
Date: ㉒ _____   _____

(AT LEAST ONE OF THE ABOVE WITNESSES MUST ALSO SIGN THE FOLLOWING DECLARATION.)

I declare under penalty of perjury under the laws of ㉔ _____ that I am not
                                                          (insert province)

related to the principal by blood, marriage or adoption, and to the best of my knowledge I am not entitled to any part of the estate of the principal upon the death of the principal under a will now existing or by operation of law.

Signature: ㉕ _____   Address: ㉘ _____
Print Name: ㉖ _____
Date: ㉗ _____   _____

COPIES: You should retain an executed copy of this document and give one to your Agent. The power of attorney should be available so a copy may be given to your providers of personal care.

POWER OF ATTORNEY
FOR PERSONAL CARE

WARNING TO PERSON EXECUTING THIS DOCUMENT

THIS IS AN IMPORTANT LEGAL DOCUMENT. IT CREATES A POWER OF ATTORNEY FOR PERSONAL CARE. BEFORE EXECUTING THIS DOCUMENT, YOU SHOULD KNOW THESE IMPORTANT FACTS:

1.   THIS DOCUMENT GIVES THE PERSON YOU DESIGNATE AS YOUR AGENT THE POWER TO MAKE PERSONAL CARE DECISIONS FOR YOU. THIS POWER IS SUBJECT TO ANY LIMITATIONS OR STATEMENTS OF YOUR DESIRES THAT YOU INCLUDE IN THIS DOCUMENT. THE POWER TO MAKE PERSONAL CARE DECISIONS FOR YOU MAY INCLUDE CONSENT, REFUSAL OF CONSENT, OR WITHDRAWAL OF CONSENT TO ANY CARE, TREATMENT, SERVICE, OR PROCEDURE TO MAINTAIN, DIAGNOSE, OR TREAT A PHYSICAL OR MENTAL CONDITION. YOU MAY STATE IN THIS DOCUMENT ANY TYPES OF TREATMENT OR PLACEMENTS THAT YOU DO NOT DESIRE.

2.   THE PERSON YOU DESIGNATE IN THIS DOCUMENT HAS A DUTY TO ACT CONSISTENT WITH YOUR DESIRES AS STATED IN THIS DOCUMENT OR OTHERWISE MADE KNOWN OR, IF YOUR DESIRES ARE UNKNOWN, TO ACT IN YOUR BEST INTERESTS.

3.   EXCEPT AS YOU OTHERWISE SPECIFY IN THIS DOCUMENT, THE POWER OF THE PERSON YOU DESIGNATE TO MAKE PERSONAL CARE DECISIONS FOR YOU MAY INCLUDE THE POWER TO CONSENT TO YOUR DOCTOR NOT GIVING TREATMENT OR STOPPING TREATMENT WHICH WOULD KEEP YOU ALIVE.

4.   UNLESS YOU SPECIFY A SHORTER PERIOD IN THIS DOCUMENT, THIS POWER WILL EXIST INDEFINITELY FROM THE DATE YOU EXECUTE THIS DOCUMENT AND, IF YOU ARE UNABLE TO MAKE PERSONAL CARE DECISIONS FOR YOURSELF, THIS POWER WILL CONTINUE TO EXIST UNTIL THE TIME WHEN YOU BECOME ABLE TO MAKE PERSONAL CARE DECISIONS FOR YOURSELF.

5.   NOTWITHSTANDING THIS DOCUMENT, YOU HAVE THE RIGHT TO MAKE MEDICAL AND OTHER PERSONAL CARE DECISIONS FOR YOURSELF SO LONG AS YOU CAN GIVE INFORMED CONSENT WITH RESPECT TO THE PARTICULAR DECISION. IN ADDITION, NO TREATMENT MAY BE GIVEN TO YOU OVER YOUR OBJECTION, AND PERSONAL CARE NECESSARY TO KEEP YOU ALIVE MAY NOT BE STOPPED IF YOU OBJECT.

6.   YOU HAVE THE RIGHT TO REVOKE THE APPOINTMENT OF THE PERSON DESIGNATED IN THIS DOCUMENT TO MAKE PERSONAL CARE DECISIONS FOR YOU BY NOTIFYING THAT PERSON OF THE REVOCATION ORALLY OR IN WRITING.

7.   YOU HAVE THE RIGHT TO REVOKE THE AUTHORITY GRANTED TO THE PERSON DESIGNATED IN THIS DOCUMENT TO MAKE PERSONAL CARE DECISIONS FOR YOU BY NOTIFYING THE TREATING PHYSICIAN, HOSPITAL, OR OTHER PROVIDER OF PERSONAL CARE ORALLY OR IN WRITING.

8.   THE PERSON DESIGNATED IN THIS DOCUMENT TO MAKE PERSONAL CARE DECISIONS FOR YOU HAS THE RIGHT TO EXAMINE YOUR MEDICAL RECORDS AND TO CONSENT TO THEIR DISCLOSURE UNLESS YOU LIMIT THIS RIGHT IN THIS DOCUMENT.

9.   THIS DOCUMENT REVOKES ANY PRIOR POWER OF ATTORNEY FOR PERSONAL CARE.

10.   IF THERE IS ANYTHING IN THIS DOCUMENT THAT YOU DO NOT UNDERSTAND, YOU SHOULD ASK A LAWYER TO EXPLAIN IT TO YOU.

1. DESIGNATION OF PERSONAL CARE AGENT.

I,_____

(insert your name)

do hereby designate and appoint:

Name:_____

Address:_____

Telephone Number:_____

as my Agent to make personal care decisions for me as authorized in this document.

> (Insert the name and address of the person you wish to designate as your Agent to make personal care decisions for you. Unless the person is also your spouse, legal guardian or the person most closely related to you by blood, **none** of the following may be designated as your Agent: (1) your treating provider of personal care, (2) an employee of your treating provider of personal care, (3) an operator of a community care or residential care facility, or (4) an employee of an operator of a community care or residential care facility.)

2. CREATION OF A POWER OF ATTORNEY FOR PERSONAL CARE.

By this document I intend to create a power of attorney by appointing the person designated above to make personal care decisions for me. This power of attorney shall not be affected by my subsequent incapacity.

3. GENERAL STATEMENT OF AUTHORITY GRANTED.

In the event that I am incapable of giving informed consent with respect to personal care decisions, I hereby grant to the Agent named above full power and authority to make personal care decisions for me before, or after my death, including: consent, refusal of consent, or withdrawal of consent to any care, treatment, service, or procedure to maintain, diagnose, or treat a physical or mental condition, subject only to the limitations and special provisions, if any, set forth in paragraph 4 or 6.

4. SPECIAL PROVISIONS AND LIMITATIONS.

> (Your Agent is not permitted to consent to any of the following: commitment to or placement in a mental health treatment facility, convulsive treatment, psychosurgery, sterilization, or abortion. If there are any other types of treatment or placement that you do not want your Agent's authority to give consent for or other restrictions you wish to place on your Agent's authority, you should list them in the space below. If you do not write any limitations, your Agent will have the broad powers to make personal care decisions on your behalf which are set forth in paragraph 3, except to the extent that there are limits provided by law.)

In exercising the authority under this power of attorney for personal care, the authority of my Agent is subject to the following special provisions and limitations:

_____

_____

_____

_____

_____

5. DURATION.

I understand that this power of attorney will exist indefinitely from the date I execute this document unless I establish a shorter time. If I am unable to make personal care decisions for myself when this power of attorney expires, the authority I have granted my Agent will continue to exist until the time when I become able to make personal care decisions for myself.

I wish to have this power of attorney end on the following date: _____

(Fill in expiration date if applicable)

6. STATEMENT OF DESIRES.

(With respect to decisions to withhold or withdraw life-sustaining treatment, your Agent must make personal care decisions that are consistent with your known desires. You can, but are not required to, indicate your desires below. If your desires are unknown, your Agent has the duty to act in your best interests; and, under some circumstances, a judicial proceeding may be necessary so that a court can determine the personal care decision that is in your best interests. If you wish to indicate your desires, you may INITIAL the statement or statements that reflect your desires and/or write your own statements in the space below.)

I direct my attending physician to withhold or withdraw life-sustaining treatment that serves only to prolong the process of my dying, if I should be in a terminal condition or in a state of permanent unconsciousness. I direct that treatment be limited to measures to keep me comfortable and to relieve pain, including any pain that might occur by withholding or withdrawing life-sustaining treatment.

In addition, if I am in the condition described above, I feel especially strong about the following forms of treatment:

I (   ) do (   ) do not want cardiac resuscitation.

I (   ) do (   ) do not want mechanical respiration.

I (   ) do (   ) do not want tube feeding or any other artificial or invasive form of nutrition (food) or hydration (water).

I (   ) do (   ) do not want blood or blood products.

I (   ) do (   ) do not want any form of surgery or invasive diagnostic tests.

I (   ) do (   ) do not want kidney dialysis.

I (   ) do (   ) do not want antibiotics.

I realize that if I do not specifically indicate my preference regarding any of the forms of treatment listed above, I may receive that form of treatment.

(If you wish to change your answer, you may do so by drawing an "X" through the answer
you do not want, and circling the answer you prefer.)

Other or Additional Statements of Desires:_____

_____

_____

_____

_____

7. DESIGNATION OF ALTERNATE AGENT.

(You are not required to designate any alternative Agent but you may do so. Any alternative Agent you designate will be able to make the same personal care decisions as the Agent designated in paragraph 1, page 2, in the event that he or she is unable or unwilling to act as your Agent. Also, if the Agent designated in paragraph 1 is your spouse, his or her designation as your Agent is automatically revoked by law if your marriage is dissolved.)

If the person designated in paragraph 1 as my Agent is unable to make personal care decisions for me, then I designate the following persons to serve as my Agent to make personal care decisions for me as authorized in this document, such persons to serve in the order listed below:

A.   First Alternative Agent

Name:_____

Address:_____

_____

Telephone Number:_____

B.   Second Alternative Agent

Name:_____

Address:_____

_____

Telephone Number:_____

8. PRIOR DESIGNATIONS REVOKED. I revoke any prior power of attorney for personal care.

(YOU MUST DATE AND SIGN THIS POWER OF ATTORNEY)

I sign my name to this Power of Attorney for Personal Care on _____

                                                                               (date)

at_____, _____

          (city)   (province)

          _____

                              (Signature)

(THIS POWER OF ATTORNEY WILL NOT BE VALID FOR MAKING PERSONAL CARE DECISIONS UNLESS IT IS SIGNED BY AT LEAST TWO QUALIFIED WITNESSES WHO ARE PERSONALLY KNOWN TO YOU AND WHO ARE PRESENT WHEN YOU SIGN.)

I declare under penalty of perjury under the laws of _____that the principal

                                                                     (insert province)

is personally known to me, that the principal signed or acknowledged this power of attorney in my presence, that the principal appears to be of sound mind and under no duress, fraud, or undue influence, that I am not the person appointed as Agent by this document, and that I am not a provider of personal care, an employee of a provider of personal care, the operator of a community care facility, nor an employee of an operator of a personal care facility.

Signature:_____   Residence Address:_____

Print Name: _____   _____

Date:_____   _____

Signature:_____   Residence Address:_____

Print Name: _____   _____

Date:_____   _____

(AT LEAST ONE OF THE ABOVE WITNESSES MUST ALSO SIGN THE FOLLOWING DECLARATION.)

I declare under penalty of perjury under the laws of _____ that I am not
                                                              (insert province)
related to the principal by blood, marriage or adoption, and to the best of my knowledge I am not
entitled to any part of the estate of the principal upon the death of the principal under a will now
existing or by operation of law.

Signature:_____   Address:_____

Print Name: _____   _____

Date:_____   _____

COPIES: You should retain an executed copy of this document and give one to your Agent. The
           power of attorney should be available so a copy may be given to your providers of
           personal care.

Glossary of useful terms

A

Administer

To manage your estate until all of the terms of the will are carried out.

Administrator

a person the court appoints to manage the probate of the estate of a person without a valid will.

Affidavit

A sworn statement under oath.

Agent

a person who acts for or in the place of another by authority from him or her.

Alternate

A contingent beneficiary or substitute representative, named to serve in case the original cannot.

Assets

Anything you own that has value.

B-D

Beneficiary

A person who inherits from you through your will. A beneficiary may also be a charity or an institution.

Bequest

A gift of property that you make in your will.

Bond

Money paid to the court by the Executor/Executrix/Trustee to ensure that he or she will administer the estate in good faith.

Codicil

An amendment to the will that changes the will in some way.

Contingent beneficiary

An alternate beneficiary.

Defame

To cause someone embarrassment or humiliation which results in a damaged reputation.

Devise

A gift of real estate, also called a bequest.

Disinherit

To deprive someone of the right to inherit in your will.

E-H

Elective share

Also called the forced share, it is the percentage of the estate that the spouse may choose instead of inheriting under the will.

Encumbrance

A legal claim, such as a mortgage, that might block the transfer of property.

Estate

All of the personal and real property that you own at death.

Executor/Executrix/Trustee

Terms for the person who executes one's will.

Gift

Any bequest that you make in your will.

Grantor

A person who gives his or her rights to another.

Guardian

The person you name to legally care for your minor children.

Healthcare provider

a doctor, nurse, hospital or aide that provides health care.

Heir

a person who inherits property, either through a will or intestate succession.

I-N

Inheritance

The gift you receive from a will.

Intestacy

Dying without a valid will.

Joint property

All property owned jointly with another party or parties.

Legal age

The age at which a minor becomes an adult. This age varies according to state law.

Libel

False written statements about another person.

Living will

A document in which you indicate at what point you no longer want medical science to prolong your life.

Living trust

A trust established while alive, also known as an inter vivos trust.

Nonmarital child

A child born out of wedlock.

Non-probate property

Property that is not considered to be part of your estate.

O-R

Operation of law

The rights and obligations that are set forth in the law; marriage and divorce, for example. These rights and obligations do not depend upon private agreements.

Probate

The process of proving in court that a will is valid and legal.

Personal property

All of the property you own, excluding real estate; also called personalty.

Power of attorney

A document authorizing another person to act on your behalf.

Principal

A person who has another act for him or her subject to his or her instruction or control; the person from whom an agent's authority derives.

Probate

The process of proving the legality and validity of a will in court.

Real property

All the real estate you own; also called realty. Real property does not include any personal property.

Remainder

The remainder of an estate after specific property has been distributed.

Residuary bequests

The remaining property that has not been distributed elsewhere in the will.

S-W

Spouse

One's husband or wife; any married person.

Testator

The person making the will if a male.

Testatrix

The person making the will if a female.

Trust

An agreement whereby one person (grantor) transfers property to a second person (trustee) to be held for the benefit of a third person (beneficiary).

Trustee

The person who holds title, manages, and distributes the trust property for the benefit of the trust beneficiary.

Valid

Legally sound, authentic.

Viatical

A financial service for the terminally ill which enables qualified individuals to obtain immediate cash from all or part of their life insurance policies.

Will

A legal document that sets forth the wishes of the testator after his or her death. This document distributes the property of the testator, and appoints representatives to administer the estate.

Witness

One who signs his or her name to a will in order to authenticate it.

Index

A-C••••

Administrator...........................20

Administrator bond 20

Adopted children clause...........87

Advance Health Care Directives Act......................................155

Alternate gift provision 83

Attribution laws........................191

Beneficiaries.............................13

Bequests....................................68

Cemetary bequest clause...........87

Charitable donations 85

Co-ownership 179

Codicil 66

Common disaster clause...........86

Common-law couples...............38

Common-law spouse.................14

Companion 24

Conditional wills......................31

Consent to Treatment and Health Care Directives Act.............152

Contesting a will.......................35

Conventional (bread & butter) wills....................................30

D-F••••

Debts...79

Dependant.................................36

Designated beneficiary assets...176

Discretionary trust 61

Disinheritance...........................81

Distributing assets....................173

Divorce agreement 40

Duties of a Power of Attorney for Personal Care 123

Duties of the Executor/Executrix/ Trustee...............................48

Escheat.....................................23

Estate plan................................13

Estate planning.......................173

Executor....................................43

Executor's year.........................49

Executrix 43

Family trusts 197

Financial assistance.................100

Funeral expense clause 88

Funeral provider 96

Funeral services........................93

G-L••••

Gift.................................189

Gift taxes.........................190

Guardian clause 69

Health Care Consent Act..........148

Health Care Directives Act 146

Healthcare providers.................115

Holographic wills 29

Hospice 127

Immovable assets.....................60

Income splitting....................196

Incorporation by reference
    clause 88

Insurable interest 199

Insurance trust.......................202

Intangible personal property.....18

Intellectual property................18

International wills...................30

Intestate............................13

Involuntary active euthanasia ..134

Involuntary passive euthanasia 134

Joint assets with right of
    survivorship......................176

Joint bank accounts 184

Jointly owned property.............66

Laws of Intestate Succession......15

Legal domicile 64

Liability 128

Life insurance 198

Life insurance proceeds............67

Life partner 24

Living trust assets 67

Living will...........................113

M-P••••

Mandatary.............................151

Mandator..............................151

Mate 24

Matrimonial possessions............39

Medical Consent Act..................151

Memorial donations...................95

Memorial societies 97

Moveable assets 60

Naming a guardian 54

Nursing home 130

Notarial wills.........................31

Per capita bequest 80

Per stirpes bequest 22, 80

Personal Directives Act.............143

Personal injury.......................128

Personal property......................17

Pour-over clause.......................89

Power of Attorney for
    Personal Care.....................114

Privileged (Serviceman) wills 30

Pre-arranged funeral 94

Preferential share 15, 22

Probate 51

Probate-free assets 187

Property under contract............67

Providing for dependents 37

Proxy 154

Prudent investor rule................21

R-S••••

Real property 19

Reciprocal wills 29

Renunciation 45

Representation Agreement Act, The 140

Residuary bequest 82

Residuary clause 71

Restriction on testamentary freedom 36

Revoking or revising a living will 163

Safekeeping your will 107

Same-sex couple 16, 38

Savings clause 89

Signing your will 106

Solely owned property 176

Solicitor 59

Special bequests 78

Substitute Health Care Decision Makers Act 146

T-W••••

Tangible property 17

Tenant-in-common 176

Testator 31

Testamentary capacity 36

Trust company 45

Trustee 43

Trustee Act 21

Types of medical treatment 162

Validity of your living will 128, 135

Voluntary active euthanasia 133

Voluntary passive euthanasia ... 133

Withholding food and fluids 134

Wills variation law 50

Wills notice 105

Witness(es) 62

Witnesses for your living will ... 162